TRANSPORTATION INFRASTRUCTURE –
ROADS, HIGHWAYS, BRIDGES, AIRPORTS AND MASS TRANSIT

ROAD INFRASTRUCTURE FUNDING

SELECTED PRACTICES AND LESSONS FROM AROUND THE GLOBE

TRANSPORTATION INFRASTRUCTURE – ROADS, HIGHWAYS, BRIDGES, AIRPORTS AND MASS TRANSIT

Additional books in this series can be found on Nova's website under the Series tab.

Additional e-books in this series can be found on Nova's website under the e-book tab.

TRANSPORTATION INFRASTRUCTURE –
ROADS, HIGHWAYS, BRIDGES, AIRPORTS AND MASS TRANSIT

ROAD INFRASTRUCTURE FUNDING

SELECTED PRACTICES AND LESSONS FROM AROUND THE GLOBE

RUSSELL T. MAY
EDITOR

nova publishers
New York

For permission to use material from this book please contact us:
Telephone 631-231-7269; Fax 631-231-8175
Web Site: http://www.novapublishers.com

Library of Congress Cataloging-in-Publication Data

ISBN: 978-1-63321-633-4

Published by Nova Science Publishers, Inc. † New York

CONTENTS

PREFACE

Chapter 1 - This report examines the funding of roads and highways in Australia, Brazil, Canada, China, England and Wales, France, Germany, Israel, Italy, Japan, Mexico, Netherlands, South Africa, and Sweden. It provides a description of the infrastructure in the jurisdiction, information on the ownership and responsibility of the roads, and taxes or other ways of collecting money to fund the nation's infrastructure.

By revealing a multiplicity of approaches to the funding of road infrastructure, the report provides an opportunity to determine whether lessons can be learned from the experiences of other countries in funding roads and highways.

Chapter 2 - Federal surface transportation programs are currently funded primarily through taxes on motor fuels that are deposited in the highway trust fund (HTF). Although there has been some modification to the tax system, the tax rates, which are fixed in terms of cents per gallon, have not been increased at the federal level since 1993. Prior to the recession that began in 2007, annual increases in driving, with a concomitant increase in fuel use, were sufficient to keep revenues rising steadily. This is no longer the case. Future increases in fuel economy standards are expected to suppress motor fuel consumption in the years ahead even if annual increases in vehicle mileage resume.

Congress has yet to address the surface transportation program's fundamental revenue issues, and has given limited legislative consideration to raising fuel taxes in recent years. Instead, Congress has financed the federal surface transportation program by supplementing fuel tax revenues with transfers from the U.S. Treasury general fund. The most recent reauthorization act, the Moving Ahead for Progress in the 21st Century Act (MAP-21; P.L.

112-141), signed by President Barack Obama on July 6, 2012, authorized spending on federal highway and public transportation programs through September 30, 2014, and provided for general fund transfers to finance the programs. MAP-21 did not address concerns about funding of surface transportation programs over the longer term.

This report begins with a discussion of the challenges facing the trust fund financing system (which supports both federal highway and public transportation programs) and then explores possible options for financing surface transportation infrastructure. Among the key points:

- Raising motor fuel taxes could provide the HTF with sufficient revenue to fully fund the program in the near term, but it may not be a viable long-term solution due to expected future declines in fuel consumption.
- Replacing current motor fuel taxes with a fuel sales tax or a fee based on vehicle miles traveled (VMT) raise a variety of financial and administrative concerns.
- Treasury general fund transfers could be used to make up for the HTF's projected shortfalls but would require budget offsets of an equal amount, as required by the January 2014 budget resolution (H.Con.Res. 25, §608).
- The political difficulty of adequately financing the HTF could lead Congress to consider the desirability of changes to maintain the trust fund system or of eliminating it altogether. Such changes might involve a reallocation of responsibilities and obligations among federal, state, and local governments.
- Interest in improving transportation infrastructure with private and non-grant funding sources, such as tolls, public-private partnerships (P3s), and federal loan programs, is increasing, but many projects may not be well suited to alternative financing.

In: Road Infrastructure Funding
Editor: Russell T. May
ISBN: 978-1-63321-633-4

Chapter 1

National Funding of Road Infrastructure*

Luis Acosta, Kelly Buchanan, Eduardo Soares, Tariq Ahmad, Laney Zhang, Clare Feikert-Ahalt, Nicolas Boring, Edith Palmer, Ruth Levush, Dante Figueroa, Sayuri Umeda, Norma C. Gutiérrez, Wendy Zeldin, Hanibal Goitom and Elin Hofverberg

Comparative Summary

Many observers of US transportation policy have called for a reevaluation of the United States's current approach to federal funding of highway infrastructure, which mostly relies on a fuel tax of 18.4 cents per gallon, an amount set in 1993. Most notably, the National Surface Transportation Infrastructure Financing Commission, after extensive review of existing studies and conducting its own research, recommended that the US transition to a user-charge system such as a vehicle-miles-traveled system.[1]

Some US states have already conducted studies with alternative funding mechanisms.[2] For example, Oregon has conducted two pilot studies on road-user fees. One study conducted in 2006–2007 found that a mileage fee could

* This is an edited, reformatted and augmented version of a report issued by the Law Library of Congress, Global Legal Research Center, March 2014.

be implemented to replace the gas tax as the principal revenue source for road funding.[3] A second pilot project conducted in 2012 found further evidence of the viability of a road usage charge administered by private-sector vendors using an easy-to-use mileage reporting and payment system.[4] Oregon is moving forward with a mileage collection system starting July 1, 2015, for five thousand volunteer motorists; the state plans to assess a charge of 1.5 cents per mile and issue a gasoline tax refund to participants.[5]

This report on the road infrastructure funding practices of foreign countries provides an opportunity to determine whether lessons can be learned from the experiences of other countries in funding roads and highways. The individual country surveys reveal a multiplicity of approaches to the funding of road infrastructure.

Several of the surveyed countries, like the US, have a fuel tax that is dedicated, at least in part, to the financing of road construction and maintenance. These include Brazil, Canada, China, Israel, and South Africa. Other countries place fuel and other excise taxes with general revenues and fund roads from general revenues, including Australia, England, Germany, Italy, and Mexico. Japan used to dedicate fuel and vehicle taxes to road infrastructure, but began placing such revenues into the general account in fiscal year 2009.

Several of the countries appear to rely somewhat heavily on private roads, concessions, or private-public partnerships as means to fund some of their road infrastructure, including Canada, China, France, Israel, and South Africa. In Australia, some state governments have developed networks of toll roads in partnership with private-sector investors, and the present Australian government is currently evaluating possible mechanisms for maximizing private-sector investment in major infrastructure projects.

Most of the surveyed countries have tolling systems to obtain part of their revenue for financing roads. In the case of Japan and France, the surveys note that tolls are linked with the weight of the vehicle and distance traveled. In the Netherlands, tolls known as "mobility rates" are charged for the use of roads as cars enter fee-payment gateways.

In England, a congestion tax is imposed on vehicles that enter central London during certain hours. Efforts to spread the congestion tax to other cities in England and Wales were abandoned, however. A congestion tax is also imposed in Sweden, in the cities of Stockholm and Gothenburg. This tax is not used for road maintenance; its purpose is to shift the preferred means of transportation from cars to public transportation, and to pay for the environmental effects of motor vehicle use.

Australia imposes a fuel-based, road-user charge on heavy trucks based on the amount of fuel used. A reform advisory group has proposed that trucks should be required to have GPS devices installed to enable taxation on the basis of distance traveled, and has argued that there should be a stronger relationship between revenues from user charges and the provision of the road network.

In France, the government was planning this year to implement a tax on heavy trucks that would have contributed to the financing of transportation infrastructure, which would have been calculated on a per-kilometer basis and on the basis of the vehicle's size, age, and level of emissions. The implementation of this tax has been postponed, perhaps until 2015, because of strong public opposition.

Sweden taxes motor vehicles to pay for costs associated with them, including carbon dioxide emissions and road maintenance. The Netherlands imposes a motor vehicle tax based on the vehicle's carbon dioxide emission level. Italy similarly imposes a vehicle tax based in part on the amount of pollution generated by the vehicle.

The Netherlands government in 2009 considered imposing a per-kilometer fee for motor vehicle use and abolishing the motor vehicle tax, but that scheme was never instituted.

In England, the prospect of a national system of road pricing based on usage was raised by a Transport Minister in 2012, but no legislation has been proposed.

In Sweden, a December 2013 government report discussing possible changes to the taxation of motor vehicles proposed a new tax on heavy-duty vehicles based on kilometers driven.

Australia

Summary

Under Australia's federal arrangements, state and local governments are responsible for road construction and maintenance. However, the federal government provides funding assistance under various programs. The federal government also collects a fuel excise tax, a Goods and Services Tax on fuel and vehicle sales, and a road user charge that applies to heavy vehicles based on fuel consumption, while state governments collect vehicle registration fees and vehicle stamp duties. Federal revenue from road transport-related activities is added to the general revenue pool and is not earmarked for road infrastructure expenditure. Rather, expenditure under the various funding programs is appropriated as part of the annual budget process. In addition to federal, state, and local revenue, private sector investment is also a source of funding for some roads, and three states maintain networks of toll roads. The current government has asked the Productivity Commission to investigate how infrastructure is currently funded and financed in Australia and to explore possible alternative mechanisms, with a particular focus on maximizing private-sector investment in major projects. A further key area for possible reform in the near future is the heavy vehicle charging system, with a reform advisory group apparently considering proposals for distance and road use charges, and for associated revenue to be directed to state and local governments to use for road infrastructure.

I. Introduction

The Commonwealth of Australia is made up of six states, two mainland territories, and several offshore territories. The Australian Constitution establishes a federal system of government.[6] Under the federal financial arrangements, all personal and corporate income tax, a value-added tax (Goods and Services Tax (GST)), excise duties, and other taxes are collected by the federal government. State and territory governments collect such taxes as land taxes, payroll taxes, motor vehicle taxes, and stamp duties. In addition, local councils levy "rates" (i.e., annual taxes) based on property values.[7] In the 2009–10 tax year, the taxation revenue of the federal government represented 80% of the taxation revenue for all levels of government. The revenue of state and territory governments is "supplemented by the distribution of grants from the Commonwealth Government, which includes the allocation of GST revenue."[8]

Under the Australian Constitution, roads are the responsibility of state and local governments. However, the federal government provides funds for the construction and maintenance of different types of road infrastructure as part of its revenue distribution arrangements.[9] The remainder of funding for various road projects comes from state and local revenue and transfers or investment from the private sector. The federal government establishes national strategies related to significant road infrastructure and distributes funding under various programs,[10] including dedicating funds to work related to a defined "National Land Transport Network" (commonly referred to as the National Network) of important road infrastructure links as well as providing funding to state and local governments for local and regional transport improvements.[11]

The Department of Infrastructure and Regional Development is the federal agency responsible for providing advice on various road transport policies and programs and administering these on behalf of the Australian government.[12] The government has also established a statutory body called Infrastructure Australia, which conducts high-level analysis and advises governments, investors, and infrastructure owners on issues such as Australia's current and future infrastructure needs and mechanisms for financing infrastructure investments.[13]

II. Fuel and Vehicle Taxes and Charges

There are a range of taxes and charges in Australia that apply to road transport-related activities, including the following:

A. Goods and Services Tax

A GST of 10% was introduced in Australia in July 2000.[14] The rate is applied to most goods sold in Australia, including transport fuels[15] and motor vehicles. GST revenue is collected from businesses by the federal government and distributed to the states in accordance with recommendations made by the Commonwealth Grants Commission.[16]

B. Fuel Tax

Australia has imposed customs and excise duties on transport fuel since the early 1900s. Unleaded petrol (i.e., gasoline) and diesel are both currently taxed at a rate of AU$0.38143 per liter (about US$1.26 per gallon).[17] Petrol excise was reduced by 6.7 cents per liter when GST was introduced in 2000, and lowered slightly further in 2001. Since 2001, the excise rate has not been indexed to inflation, and the rate has not been changed since that time.[18] Fuel tax credits are available to businesses in relation to certain fuels and uses,[19] as well as in relation to taxable fuel acquired for use in domestic (i.e., household) energy generation and nonprofit emergency vehicles.[20]

C. Luxury Car Tax

A luxury car tax[21] (LCT) of 33% is "imposed on the GST-inclusive value of luxury cars over the relevant LCT threshold."[22] The current threshold is

AU$75,375 (about US$65,670) for fuel- efficient cars and AU$60,316 (about US$52,550) for other cars.[23]

D. Heavy Vehicle Charges

Owners of heavy vehicles are required to pay a registration charge as well as a fuel-based road user charge in order to ensure that heavy vehicles "pay for their fair share of road spending."[24] Under the current arrangements, trucking operators can receive a fuel tax credit for the difference between the road user charge and the fuel excise rate.[25]

Identical registration charges are established through regulations enacted in all states and territories and are adjusted annually in accordance with an annual adjustment formula that was established by the Model Heavy Vehicle Charges Act 2007.[26] This formula involves the application of a seven-year average for both road expenditure and vehicle numbers.

Changes to the road user charge are calculated by the National Transport Commission (NTC) using the same factor that is applied to adjust the registration charge, and the NTC must also act in accordance with the principles set by the National Standing Council on Transport and Infrastructure and the Council of Australian Governments.[27] Under the Fuel Tax Act 2006 (Cth), the federal government must undertake a consultation process on proposed changes to the road user charge.[28]

Beginning July 1, 2013, the rates of both charges were increased by 2.5% to reflect changes in the level of expenditure on roads. The current road-user charge is AU$0.2614 per liter (about US$0.86 per gallon),[29] while the registration charge varies depending on the type of vehicle.[30] For example, the charge for a two-axle truck up to twelve tons is AU$556 (about US$485), while the charge for a "long combination truck" is AU$9,595 (about US$8,365).[31] The registration fees are collected by the states and territories[32] and road user charges are collected by the federal government.

A Heavy Vehicle Charging and Investment Reform project, established by the Council of Australian Governments, will continue in 2014.[33] The reform advisory group's current proposals reportedly indicate that in the future trucks may be required to have GPS devices installed so that they can be charged for distances traveled and roads used.[34]

E. Other Vehicle Registration Charges and Stamp Duty

All Australian states and territories require private vehicle owners to pay an annual registration fee in order to use public roads. Unlike the national vehicle registration system for heavy vehicles described above, the fee amount for cars varies by state as well as by type of vehicle. The total fee may also reflect different components, such as a charge for compulsory third-party insurance (e.g., in South Australia,[35] Queensland,[36] Victoria,[37] and the Northern Territory[38]).

In addition to the registration fee, a stamp duty (variously called, e.g., "vehicle registration duty," "motor vehicle duty," or "vehicle licence duty") is payable to the relevant state authority when a person registers a new motor vehicle or when transferring a registration to another person.[39]

F. Tolls

Some state governments have developed networks of toll roads, often in partnership with private- sector investors. Toll roads are primarily situated in major metropolitan areas in the east of the country (New South Wales,[40] Victoria,[41] and Queensland[42]).

III. National Road Infrastructure Funding

A. History

In 1959, the government announced the "termination of the hypothecation arrangements [i.e., earmarks] for road funding."[43] The policy of funding road infrastructure from general revenue rather than earmarked funds continued until 1982, when the Australian Bicentennial Road Development Trust Fund Act was enacted, establishing a road development program funded by a surcharge of AU$0.01 per liter (later AU$0.02 per liter) on the excise of petrol and diesel. The program was replaced by the Australian Land Transport Development Act 1988,[44] which abolished the surcharge and allowed the government to determine what share of excise on petrol and diesel should be paid into a trust fund for the purpose of funding road projects under the Act. Although this Act is still in force, since the 1991–92 fiscal year "successive Governments have set road funding in the budget process, discontinuing the practice of hypothecating a proportion of fuel excise to roads."[45]

B. Current Federal Funding Programs

Under the current road funding arrangements at the federal level, revenue from the fuel excise tax and other road transport-related federal taxes or charges is added to the general revenue pool (the Consolidated Revenue Fund[46]) and is not earmarked or placed in designated funds for road (or other transport) infrastructure projects.[47] Federal expenditure related to road infrastructure is therefore funded by appropriations as part of the annual budget process. This includes payments to states and territories for road infrastructure projects that come under the "Nation Building Program,"[48] which is part of the "National Partnership Payments to the States" distribution system agreed upon between the federal and state governments.[49] Funding under this program is appropriated through a "special account" appropriation mechanism authorized by the Nation- building Funds Act 2008 (Cth).[50] Allocations under the relevant fund are guided by an infrastructure priority list developed by Infrastructure Australia.[51]

The following are some of the major funding programs specifically related to road infrastructure that are administered by the Department of Infrastructure and Regional Development as part of its broader "Infrastructure Investment" program.[52]

1. National Projects

This program "targets projects on the National Network that will deliver the highest benefits to the nation."[53] It involves the distribution of funds to individual states for major road works that will "significantly improve the efficiency and safety of the National Network."[54]

2. Off-Network Projects

Under this program, funds are provided to state, territory, and local governments for road projects not on the National Network.[55]

3. Roads to Recovery Program

This program involves the allocation and direct payment of funds to local authorities in each state and territory to support the "maintenance of the nation's local road infrastructure asset."[56] Each council is guaranteed a share of the available funding and nominates projects to be funded.[57] Funding is then distributed "according to a formula based on population and road length set by the Local Government Grants Commissions in each state and the Northern Territory."[58] General conditions apply related to expenditure of payments under the program as well as planning and reporting.[59]

4. Funding for Local Roads

Unlike the Roads to Recovery program, this program provides untied local road grants to councils as part of annual financial assistance grants.[60] The local road grants program reflects the following features:

- The amount provided is increased annually to compensate for both population growth and inflation.
- Each State receives a fixed share of the grant; the share being set out in legislation.
- Each council's share of the grant is determined by the State's local government grants commission.
- The grants are untied.
- South Australian councils also receive supplementary funding for local roads in addition to their financial assistance grants.[61]

5. Black Spot Program

Projects funded under this program include various measures aimed at addressing issues at road locations where many accidents are occurring.[62] Individuals and organizations are able to nominate a "black spot" for funding consideration, and these are assessed by the relevant state authority and state "Consultative Panels" before being submitted to the federal government.[63] In order to be eligible for funds, project proposals must include information on whether there have been a minimum number of casualty crashes at the road or site and "should be able to demonstrate a benefit to cost ratio of at least 2:1."[64]

IV. Future Direction

A change in the federal administration occurred in September 2013 with the election of the center-right Coalition led by Tony Abbott of the Liberal Party, who became Prime Minister. Part of the Coalition's election platform was to pursue a "significant infrastructure agenda" involving AU$5 billion in additional funding, including funding for several major road projects.[65]

In November 2013, the Prime Minister, the Treasurer, and the Assistant Minister for Infrastructure and Regional Development announced that the Australian Productivity Commission would be tasked with analyzing and reporting on the following areas:

- How infrastructure is currently funded and financed in Australia, including by the Commonwealth, the States and the private sector;
- The rationale, role and objectives of alternative funding and financing mechanisms;

- Examine the cost structure of major infrastructure projects in Australia, including where infrastructure project costs have increased considerably, compared with other countries;
- Provide advice on ways to improve decision-making and implementation processes to facilitate a reduction in the cost of public infrastructure projects; and
- Comment on other relevant policy measures, including any non-legislative approaches, which would help ensure effective delivery of infrastructure services over both the short and long term.[66]

The Productivity Commission subsequently released a detailed Issues Paper and received a number of submissions from interested parties.[67] It is set to release a draft report in March 2014 and will then hold public hearings before submitting a final report to the government in May 2014.[68] A major part of the discussion, and a "key plank" in the government's approach, relates to possible mechanisms for maximizing private sector investment in major infrastructure projects, including roads.[69] In January 2014, *The Australian* reported that various submissions to the Productivity Commission called for greater direct charging of all road users through tolls.[70]

There is considerable information and analysis available related to private investment in infrastructure in Australia. As indicated above, various states have previously examined and utilized different private funding mechanisms for the development of road infrastructure, including Public Private Partnerships and the use of tolls. In 2008, the Council of Australian Governments endorsed the National Public Private Partnership Policy and Guidelines for use by all state and territory governments.[71]

In 2011, a report prepared for the Department of Infrastructure and Transport (as it was then called) found that "over-optimistic patronage forecasts have contributed to the commercial failure of a series of major toll roads in Australia."[72] The Department then undertook further examination of the issues and potential solutions for managing patronage forecasting.[73]

In 2013, Reuters reported that the Queensland government was considering selling its toll road business to "capitalise on strong demand for the country's infrastructure assets."[74] The approach of initially publicly funding the building of toll roads, including through borrowing money, and then later selling the project to private investors was also being considered for a project in New South Wales.[75] Most recently, it was reported that China Merchants Group, one of China's biggest state-owned enterprises, "is eyeing investment opportunities in Australia as state governments look to privatise assets such as toll roads and other infrastructure to reduce debt."[76]

In addition to possible changes in the use of various public and private financing mechanisms under the new government, future reforms appear likely to include changes to the heavy vehicle charging system discussed above, depending on the outcomes of recommendations made by the Heavy Vehicle Investment and Charging Reform group. Furthermore, according to the group's submission to the Productivity Commission, it is "strongly of the view that there must be a stronger relationship between the revenues associated with user charges and the provision of the road network. That is, heavy vehicle charges revenues should flow back to road providers as a source of funding for road provision and maintenance."[77] The reform proposals will apparently be considered at the next meeting of the Council of Australian Governments, which is likely to be held around April 2014.[78]

BRAZIL

Summary

The Brazilian federal government administers a federal transportation system, which is implemented through federal agencies or by concession, authorization, or lease to a public or private enterprise, or to a public-private partnership. Regardless of the type of administration, the federal government is authorized to apply financial resources to the system.

In 2001, a new federal agency subordinated to the Ministry of Transportation was created to implement the policies formulated for administering the infrastructure of the federal transportation system, including the operation, maintenance, servicing or replacement, adjustment of capacity, and expansion of the infrastructure through the building of new roads and terminals.

A federal tax levied on the import and sale of oil and oil products, natural gas and its derivatives, and ethanol fuel was instituted in 2001 to finance, among other things, transportation infrastructure programs. Twenty-nine percent of the collected proceeds must be delivered to the states and the Federal District, which are obligated to apply these funds to the financing of transportation infrastructure programs. The states must, in turn, deliver 25% of the funds allocated to them to their municipalities, to be used in the financing of transportation infrastructure programs. Brazil is not contemplating the enactment of a vehicle-miles-traveled tax.

I. Road Infrastructure

A. National System of Transportation

Article 1 of Law No. 12,379 of January 6, 2011, provides for the National System of Transportation (Sistema Nacional de Viação, SNV),[79] in accordance with subsections XII and XXI of article 21 of the Federal Constitution,[80] which determines that the federal government (*União*) has the power to operate, directly or through authorization, concession, or permission, the services of interstate and international passenger transportation by road. There are transportation systems at three levels: the federal, state, and municipal level. These systems encompass not only road traffic but also rail, waterway, and air transportation. Of these, the federal system is administered by the SNV.[81]

B. Federal System of Transportation

The SFV is composed of the Federal Highway Subsystem, Federal Railroad Subsystem, Federal Waterway Subsystem, and Federal Airway Subsystem.[82] The administration of the SFV belongs to the federal government and involves the planning, construction, maintenance, operation, and exploitation of its components.[83]

The federal government must exercise its powers related to the SFV directly through federal agencies and organs,[84] or by concession, authorization, or lease to a public or private enterprise,[85] or to a public-private partnership.[86] The federal government may apply financial resources to the SFV, whatever the system of administration is adopted.[87]

II. Funding for National Road Infrastructure

Highway construction and maintenance is essentially funded by the federal government through tolls, concessions, and taxation imposed on the import and sale of oil and oil products, natural gas and its derivatives, and ethanol fuel.

A. Tolls

Article 150(V) of the Constitution prohibits the federal government, the states, the Federal District, and the municipalities from establishing limitations on the movement of persons or goods by means of interstate or intercounty taxes, except for the collection of tolls for the use of government-maintained highways.[88]

B. Concessions

The government may grant concessions for the construction and operation of federal highways and the operation of road projects, as well as for the operation and administration of existing highways through toll collection.[89]

Law No. 8,987 of February 10, 2005, regulates the concession of public services and public works, and the permission to render public services, both of which must be governed by the terms of article 175 of the Constitution,[90] by Law No. 8,987, by the relevant legal standards, and by the clauses of all indispensable contracts.[91]

The government is authorized, through the Ministry of Transportation, to delegate, for a period of up to twenty-five years and renewable for up to twenty-five more years, to municipalities, states, and the Federal District, or to a consortium between them, the administration of highways, exploitation of stretches of highway, or development of federal road projects.[92] The delegation must be formalized through an agreement (*convênio*),[93] which must have a clause providing for the possibility of enforcing the laws of the municipality, the state, or the Federal District regarding the charging of tolls or port tariffs, or other form of collection, as long as it is not contrary to federal law.[94] The income generated from such charges must be applied to additional works, improvements, expansion of the traffic capacity, preservation, and signs and signals on the highway on which it is charged, and on road sections that give access to the highway.[95]

The federal government may allocate financial resources to a concessionaire for the construction, maintenance, improvement, and operation of highways, portions of highways, federal road projects, or federal ports, provided that such projects and services are not the responsibility of the concessionaire.[96]

On June 5, 2001, Law No. 10,233 created the National Department of Transportation Infrastructure (Departamento Nacional de Infraestrutura de Transportes, DNIT), a federal agency subordinated to the Ministry of Transportation and charged with the duty of implementing the policies formulated for administering the infrastructure of the SFV, including the operation, maintenance, servicing or replacement, adjustment of capacity, and expansion of the infrastructure through the building of new roads and terminals, according to the principles and guidelines established in Law No. 10,233.[97]

C. Revenue from Taxes

1. Law No. 10,336 of December 19, 2001

Law No. 10,336 of December 19, 2001 created the Contribution of Intervention in the Economic Domain (*Contribuição de Intervenção no Domínio Econômico*, CIDE), a tax levied on the import and sale of oil and oil products, natural gas and its derivatives, and ethanol fuel.[98]

The proceeds from the collection of the CIDE will be allocated, according to the budgetary law, for subsidizing the prices or transportation of ethanol, natural gas and its derivatives, and petroleum products; the financing of environmental projects related to the oil and gas industry; and the financing of transportation infrastructure programs.[99]This revenue finances not only federal highways but also state and municipal highways and roads.[100]

The CIDE is triggered by the import and domestic sale, by the contributors mentioned in article 2, of gasoline and its chains;[101] diesel and its chains; aviation kerosene and other kerosene; fuel oil; liquefied petroleum fuels, including those derived from natural gas and naphtha; and ethanol fuel.[102] The following specific CIDE rates apply to the import and domestic sale of

I. gasoline, R$860,00 [approximately US$358.33] per cubic meter;
II. diesel, R$390,00 [US$162.50] per cubic meter;
III. aviation kerosene, R$92,10 [US$38.37] per cubic meter;
IV. other kerosene, R$92,10 (US$38.37) per cubic meter;
V. fuel oil with high sulfur content R$40,90 [US$17.04] per ton;
VI. fuel oil with low sulfur content R$40,90 [US$17.04] per ton;
VII. liquefied gas derived from petroleum, including that derived from natural gas and naphtha, R$250,00 [US$104.16] per ton; [and]
VIII. ethanol fuel, R$37,20 [US$15.50] per cubic meter.[103]

2. Law No. 10,636 of December 30, 2002

Law No. 10,636 of December 30, 2002, established the criteria and guidelines for the application of funds raised through the CIDE, pursuant to the terms of Constitutional Amendment No. 33 of December 11, 2001, which amended articles 149 and 177 of the Constitution. Law No. 10,636 also created the National Fund for Transportation Infrastructure (Fundo Nacional de Infra- Estrutura de Transportes, FNIT).[104]

The application of CIDE funds to programs of transportation infrastructure must have as key objectives reducing automotive fuel consumption, achieving the most economical way to meet the demand for the transport of people and goods, ensuring the safety and comfort of users, decreasing the travel time of public transportation users, improving the quality of life of the population, and reducing inefficiency in the use of productive resources. These objectives must be achieved despite the increase in the cost of building urban centers and with the lowest possible transportation and port/terminal costs in the domestic use and export of consumer products.[105]

The FNIT, which is subordinated to the Ministry of Transportation, was created for the purpose of financing transportation infrastructure investment programs.[106] FNIT funds must have a multimodal application, according to the annual budget law, and meet the objectives established in article 6 of Law No. 10,636.[107] Article 12 of Law No. 10,636 determines that the administration of the federal road infrastructure and the operation of transportation under the control of the federal government must preferably be performed in a decentralized manner, promoting their transfer, where possible, to public entities and to other entities of the federation through delegation, or to the private sector through concession, permission, or authorization, provided that the corresponding legislation is respected.[108]

II. New Initiatives on Road Infrastructure

Law No. 10,336 of 2001 was the last legislative initiative designed to raise funds for highway infrastructure. In this regard, Brazil is not currently contemplating the enactment of taxation based on the miles traveled by a vehicle.

CANADA

Summary

Under Canada's Constitution Act, the provinces and territories have exclusive jurisdiction over the building and maintenance of national highways.

Local and municipal roads are under the jurisdiction of municipal governments. The federal government administers a number of federal funds to assist with road infrastructure projects, many of which are structured through bilateral cost-sharing agreements with specific provinces, territories or municipal governments for specific projects. Most of the monies for these various funds come from consolidated revenue, which is then allocated through a budgetary process. However, part of the federal gas tax revenue is earmarked for municipal infrastructure projects under the Federal Gas Tax Fund.

Provincially, the general practice is not to tie fuel taxes to highway or road infrastructure projects. In most provinces, expenditure on highway infrastructure projects is allocated under a government budget from the general revenue rather than from a particular tax source. Public-private partnerships have also been utilized to fund major road infrastructure projects.

I. Introduction

Under the *Constitution Act, 1867, the provinces and territories of Canada are exclusively responsible for enacting legislation on "Local Works and Undertakings," which includes* highways.[109] According to Transport Canada, provincial and territorial governments are responsible for the "planning, design, construction, operation, maintenance and financing of highways within their jurisdiction."[110] Nonetheless, the federal government contributes to funding for highway or road construction projects under specific legislation or programs of departments and agencies.[111] Local road infrastructure is largely under the jurisdiction of local municipalities, which receive a large portion of their revenue through property taxes. However, they also receive funding assistance, typically through tax transfer agreements, from both the federal and provincial governments.

II. National Road Infrastructure Funding

A. Federal Funding

Canada's approach to federal government assistance for highway infrastructure funding has historically been described as ad hoc as opposed to long-term.[112] There does not appear to be a dedicated federal tax that only supports building and/or maintenance of national highways or roads.

As noted above, although "highways are the responsibility of the provinces and territories, the federal government has a long history of providing assistance for highway construction in Canada."[113] Federal taxes, including the excise tax on gasoline and diesel fuel, go into the general coffers and help sustain a number of federal programs. Federally funded infrastructure programs that assist in funding highways and roads, as detailed below, are primarily structured through bilateral cost-sharing agreements with specific provinces and territories. The majority of these infrastructure funds are administered by Infrastructure Canada.

In 2007, the federal government of Canada launched a *Building Canada Plan*, which aimed to provide "$33 billion in stable, flexible and predictable funding to provinces, territories and municipalities, allowing them to plan for the longer-term and address their ongoing infrastructure needs."[114] Some of the funds created under the Plan that are still accepting applications and are not set to wind down include the Federal Gas Tax Fund, Building Canada Fund, and Provincial- Territorial Base Fund.

1. Federal Gas Tax Fund

Two billion[115] of the approximately five billion[116] dollars in revenue the federal government receives annually from the Federal Gas Tax is allocated to the Federal Gas Tax Fund. The Fund supports municipal infrastructure projects, which can include building and maintaining local municipal roads. According to Infrastructure Canada,

> [e]very municipality in Canada receives a portion of the Fund. The funding allocation is determined at the provincial or territorial level based on population. Funding is provided up front, twice a year to provincial and territorial governments or to the municipal associations which deliver this funding within a province, as well as to Toronto. Projects are chosen locally and prioritized according to the infrastructure needs of each community. Municipalities can pool, bank and borrow against this funding, providing significant financial flexibility.[117]

2. Building Canada Fund

The Building Canada Fund works by "making investments in public infrastructure owned by provincial, territorial and municipal governments, and in certain cases, private sector and non- profit organizations. Funding is allocated to each province and territory based on population."[118] The Building Canada Fund is a cost-shared contribution program with a "maximum federal contribution to any single project being 50 per cent."[119] The Fund's aim is to "build a stronger Canadian economy by investing in infrastructure projects that contribute to increased trade, efficient movement of goods and people, and economic growth."[120] One of the categories of investments that support economic growth includes the National Highway System.[121]

3. Provincial-Territorial Base Fund

The Provincial-Territorial Base Fund is a Can$2.275 billion fund that "provides predictable funding to provinces and territories to address core infrastructure priorities."[122] It also requires the recipient to "sign a Provincial-Territorial Base Fund Agreement with the Government of Canada."[123] According to Infrastructure Canada, "[t]o receive funding, provinces and territories must submit a capital plan containing a list of initiatives for federal cost-sharing. The plan includes a brief description of each initiative, the eligible category of investment and the total eligible cost. The federal government will contribute up to 50 per cent of the plan's eligible costs for provinces and up to 75 per cent for territories."[124]

4. Other Funds

The following funds have stopped accepting applications and will be winding down in the next few years.

a. Canada Strategic Infrastructure Fund

The Canada Strategic Infrastructure Fund (CSIF) is a cost-shared contribution program for large- scale infrastructure projects, which comprises five categories of investments. Highway infrastructure is included in the investment category that supports "large-scale projects that facilitate the movement of goods and people on Canada's National Highway System – or highways that connect to the system."[125] The projects are said to be "[in] support of sustaining the economic growth and enhancing the quality of life for Canadians."[126] The federal government can contribute up to a maximum of 50% of the total eligible costs of the projects. Projects are typically "chosen according to regional and national infrastructure priorities,"[127] in consultation with provinces, territories, and municipal governments as well as the private sector.[128] Moreover, funding is delivered through negotiated agreements with provincial, territorial or local governments as well as nongovernmental organizations, private companies and individuals.[129] The CSIF was established under the Canada Strategic Infrastructure Fund Act.[130]

b. Border Infrastructure Fund

The Border Infrastructure Fund (BIF) is also a cost-shared contribution program that funds "infrastructure projects that help sustain and increase the long-term efficiency of the Canada-US border."[131] The focus is on projects at or near the busiest Canada-US border crossings. The Canadian government has contributed up to a maximum of 50% of total eligible costs.

III. Provincial Road Infrastructure Funding

It appears that provincial-level fuel taxes and other road-related fees (including motor vehicle licensing and registry fees) and fines contribute to covering a large portion of highway-related construction and maintenance costs. However, in most provincial jurisdictions the fuel taxes flow into the general revenues and highway infrastructure funding is not necessarily tied to any specific revenue source. Nova Scotia is an exception, as under the Public Highways Act all revenue from its provincial gas tax and from fees and fines that are to be paid to the Department of Transportation is dedicated to a provincial highway fund.[132] In addition, in Ontario, "[p]rovince-wide, fuel taxes and other fees cover between 70 and 90 per cent of annual road construction, maintenance and policing costs."[133]

Historically, Canada has not made significant use of tolls/congestion charges and other road pricing mechanisms. However, there is increasing recognition that the gas tax base is shrinking, and major municipal governments like Vancouver are increasingly considering various road-pricing mechanisms to help fund transportation infrastructure projects.[134]

No information was found concerning usage of vehicle kilometers traveled (VKT) taxes or charges at the federal or provincial level. However, some reports indicate that VKT charges are being proposed at the municipal level, to help fund transportation and transit projects.[135]

IV. Public-Private Partnership Funding

Canada appears to heavily utilize public-private partnerships (P3s) to fund major infrastructure projects, including roads and highways. According to a report by the Fraser Institute, "[c]umulatively, Canada has planned, underway, or completed the sixth greatest number of transportation P3 projects in the OECD from 1985 to 2013 (as of Jan. 30)."[136] Moreover, "on a cost basis,

Canada's cumulative transportation P3s total ninth highest. Of the various types of transportation, including roads, rail, airports, and seaports, transportation P3s in Canada are most concentrated in roads, both in terms of number and cost."[137] Early examples of the use of P3s at the provincial level is the building of Highway 104 project[138] and Ontario Highway 407.[139]

In February 2009, the federal government of Canada established PPP Canada, a federal Crown corporation, whose mandate is to "improve the delivery of public infrastructure by achieving better value, timeliness and accountability to taxpayers, through P3s."[140] More specifically PPP Canada provides "expertise and advice in assessing and executing P3 opportunities at the federal level."[141]

PPP Canada also manages a $1.2 billion P3 Canada fund, which provides funding on a merit- basis for infrastructure projects that are procured by public authorities (including provincial, territorial, and municipal governments) through P3s.[142]

PEOPLE'S REPUBLIC OF CHINA

Summary

Funding for road construction and maintenance in China derives from a combination of government and commercial sources. Only a small share of funding has been provided by central government budgetary revenue. A 10% vehicle purchase tax is collected on the purchase of vehicles; revenue of the special taxation is dedicated to road development projects. Tolling is widely allowed, which is believed to have enabled rapid expansion of the country's road system over the last two decades.

Effective 2009, a fuel tax reform abolished road maintenance fees, which had been a stable source of funding for road maintenance.. The reform also significantly increased the oil product consumption tax, revenue from which is to be used not only to substitute the road maintenance fees, but also for several other purposes.

I. Introduction

Under the Highway Law of the People's Republic of China (Highway Law), funding of road construction may come from

- appropriations made by various levels of government, including those deriving from special funds collected through taxation;
- loans from domestic and foreign banks or foreign governments;
- investment made by domestic or foreign economic organizations;
- funds raised from enterprises and individuals to build highways (which must be on voluntary basis as required by the Highway Law); and
- funds raised through other means that conform to laws or regulations of the State Council[143]

Tolling revenue is required by law to be limited to highway uses.[144] According to the Highway Law, upon approval, tolling is allowed for highways built with loans, funds raised from enterprises and individuals, and investment made by economic organizations[145]

In practice, toll financing has been used widely, which is believed to have enabled rapid expansion of the country's road system over the last two decades.[146] Only a small share of funding has been provided by central government budgetary revenue. According to the Ministry of Transport, in the year 2012, a total of RMB1112.490 billion (about US$183.93 billion) was invested in highway construction nationwide. Only 1.8% of the overall funding came from central government budgetary revenue, and 17% from vehicle purchase tax (VPT) revenue. Local government self-financing counted for 33%, domestic loans 36.4%, and foreign investment 0.4%.[147]

Before 2009, road maintenance fees (RMFs) were collected from owners of vehicles for the maintenance, repair, technology reform and improvement, and administration of highways, based on the rational of "who uses, maintains."[148] The RMFs was abolished along with five other road- use surcharges during a fuel tax reform plan that was implemented from 2009.[149]

II. Tolls

A. Toll Roads

Under the Regulations on Administration of Toll Roads, upon approval and in accordance with the laws, tolls may be collected from users of

- Government-repaying-loan highways: highways constructed by a competent department for transportation under a local government through a loan or funds raised from enterprises or individuals; and

- Commercially operated highways: highways constructed with investments provided by domestic or foreign economic organizations, or highways with the right to collect tolls on government-repaying-loan highways assigned to such organizations.[150]

B. Limits on Lengths of Toll Collecting

The number of years that tolls can be collected for each toll road is subject to approval and is limited by law to a maximum period of time, as follows:

- For government-repaying-loan highways, fifteen years, which may be extended to twenty years for those highways located in a central or western province.
- For commercially operated highways, twenty-five years, which may be extended to thirty years for those highways located in a central or western province.[151]

III. Vehicle Purchase Tax

The Chinese vehicle purchase tax (VPT) is a special tax dedicated to road development projects. It provides a stable funding source for road development (17% in 2012). According to statistics released by the Ministry of Finance, the VPT revenue in 2013 was RMB259.6 billion (about US$42.9 billion).[152]

A. Vehicle Purchase Surcharges

A 10% surcharge on purchasing vehicles was first created in 1985. According to the document creating the vehicle purchase surcharge, the entire income from the surcharges must be used to fund the country's road development.[153]

B. Taxable Vehicles and Rate

On January 1, 2001, the surcharge was replaced by a formal VPT. Vehicles subject to the tax include automobiles, motorcycles, electric vehicles, trailers, and transport vehicles for agricultural use.[154]

The VPT rate remains 10% on the taxable price of vehicles,[155] to be paid in a lump sum within sixty days after the date of purchase and before a vehicle is registered.[156]

According to the regulations governing the VPT, the tax is levied only once on each vehicle, so that purchasing a vehicle for which a VPT has been paid is not subject to the tax for a second time.[157]

C. Collecting Authority and Uses of Tax Revenue

The VPT is collected by the central government, and allocated to local governments to fund road-development projects.[158] In addition to construction projects for roads, bridges, and tunnels, construction projects for road passenger and cargo hubs (including logistics parks (areas zoned for purposes relating to logistics) and inland waterways may also be funded by VPT revenue.[159]

Annual revenues from the VPT have grown steadily in recent years, primarily due to the rapid increase in vehicle ownership. According to a report by the Asian Development Bank, it increased from RMB21.6 billion (about US$331 million) in 2000 to RMB116.4 billion (about USD$17.8 billion) in 2009, of which about 90% was used for highway-related purposes.[160]

IV. Fuel Tax Reform

A. Road Maintenance Fees

Road Maintenance Fees (RMFs) used to be a stable source of funding for road maintenance. RMF revenue was dedicated to highway maintenance, repair, technology reform and improvement, and administration, according to the Provisions on the Administration of Collection of Road Maintenance Fee.[161]

B. Fuel Tax Reform

The central government had been contemplating a fuel tax reform for many years in order to address several policy issues, including: (1) concerns arising from collecting RMFs, which were collected by various local governments with a wide variety of fee levels, and toll road charges; (2) demand for oil, which is rapidly rising; and (3) environmental concerns, etc.[162] As early as in 2000, when the government decided to replace the vehicle purchase surcharges with the VPT, a fuel tax reform was also proposed to replace the RMFs and other road use surcharges with a new fuel tax.[163]

However, when the State Council released the final fuel tax reform plan in late 2008 after several years of contentious debate, it significantly marked up the rate of the existing consumption tax on oil products instead of creating a new fuel tax.[164] Under the final fuel tax reform plan, which took effect on January 1, 2009:

- the RMFs, waterway conservation fees, road transport management fees, road passenger and freight surcharges, water transportation management fees, and water passenger and freight surcharges were abolished; and
- the rate of the existing consumption tax on oil products was raised by RMB0.8 (about US$0.13) per liter for gasoline, RMB0.7 (about US$0.12) for diesel, and corresponding amounts for other oil products.[165]

C. New Oil Product Consumption Tax (Fuel Tax)

1. Tax Rates

The consumption tax on oil products is assessed as a fixed amount per liter.[166] Prior to the fuel tax reform, the consumption tax per liter on gasoline was RMB0.2 (about US$0.03) and on diesel RMB0.1 (about US$0.02), which was "fairly negligible."[167] The new rates of consumption tax on oil products are shown in the table below.

2. Collection

Unlike the previous RMFs, which were collected by various local governments, the new fuel tax is a central tax collected by the State Administration of Taxation (and Customs in cases of imports). The tax is currently imposed on the manufacturers and importers of oil products.[168]

3. Uses of Tax Revenue

The newly-raised revenue from the oil product consumption tax will first be used as a substitute for RMFs and other road-use charges that were abolished by the reform, according to the reform plan.[169] A significant factor of the fuel tax reform is that, under the reform plan, authorization for current and future tolls on Class II Highways[170] will gradually be removed. Accordingly, revenue from the new fuel tax will also be used to compensate for the loss of the toll fees from these roads. The fuel tax reform plan also pledged to subsidize grain producers, the poor, and public welfare sectors.[171]

England and Wales

Summary

Roads in England were built and maintained through statutory labor, tolls, and ultimately taxes raised from vehicles paid into a specific fund to provide roads. All of these methods of funding and maintaining roads ultimately failed through corruption or misapplication of funds. Currently, all taxes and duties obtained from vehicle taxes and excise duties on fuel are paid directly into the government's main fund, and monies provided for roads are allocated from the budget. The government has announced that it will likely need to reconsider how vehicles are taxed, given the advances in technology that are reducing the amount of taxes collected through traditional methods; however, it has yet to propose any changes.

I. Introduction

The United Kingdom of Great Britain and Northern Ireland is comprised of England, Wales, Scotland, and Northern Ireland. The four countries have recently undergone a period of devolution, with the power to legislate in certain areas reverting back to Scotland, Northern Ireland, and Wales. Transportation is a "reserved matter," meaning that Scotland, Wales, and Northern Ireland have the ability to legislate and create policy independently in this area. This report focuses on England, with the exception of the subheading relating to heavy vehicles, as the levy on these vehicles applies across the UK.

Road funding has a long history in England, dating back to the well-constructed and well- maintained roads of the Romans. England and Wales currently have a sizeable network of roads, and funding is currently provided at two different levels. The major roads (the strategic road network) are funded by the central government and managed by the Highways Agency. Local roads, on the other hand, are the responsibility of local authorities. The maintenance and improvement of these roads are funded through local council taxes, fees, and central government grants.

II. History of Road Funding

The history of roads in England dates back many centuries to Ley Lines, which were simple, straight trackways of rudimentary construction. In 43 AD, the invasion of the Romans led to the construction of "Roman roads," many of which are still in use today. However, after the Romans left, the roads were left unmaintained and in disrepair until the late thirteenth century, when local councils stepped in and repaired some of these roads.[172] The Highways Act 1555[173] saw the first attempt to create a statutory responsibility to provide for road upkeep. The Act put responsibility for the maintenance of roads on local parishes, imposing a statutory duty on each man with a team of horses to provide labor for six days annually for road upkeep.[174] In 1654 parishes were provided the power to collect money through levying a local rate (tax) to supplement the labor provided by the horses for the upkeep of roads.[175] The standards of road maintenance across England varied greatly and, as most travel was local, parishes focused solely on local roads. In 1835, the system of statutory labor was abandoned as it was considered largely ineffective, and parishes were expected to maintain roads "solely through a local rate."[176]

Table. New Rates of Consumption Tax on Oil Products

Tax Category	Tax Rate
Oil Product:	
1. Gasoline	
(i) Unleaded gasoline	RMB1.0 (US$0.17)/Liter
(ii) Leaded gasoline	RMB1.4 (US$0.23)/Liter
2. Diesel	RMB0.8 (US$0.13)/Liter
3. Airplane kerosene	RMB0.8 (US$0.13)/Liter
4. Naphtha	RMB1.0 (US$0.17)/Liter
5. Solvents	RMB1.0 (US$0.17)/Liter
6. Lubricants	RMB1.0 (US$0.17)/Liter
7. Fuel Oil	RMB0.8 (US$0.13)/Liter

Source: Notice of the Ministry of Finance and State Administration of Taxation on Raising Oil Product Consumption Tax (Cai Shui [2008] No. 167, issued Dec. 19, 2008, effective Jan. 1, 2009), http://www.chinatax.gov. cn/n8136506/n8136593/ n8137537/n8138502/8734242.html.

The Industrial Revolution and the increase of travel by stagecoach led to the expansion of travel and an increase in trade. Between 1720 and 1840, 1.1

million Turnpike Trusts were created, providing 32,000 kilometers of road.[177] The Turnpike Trusts charged users tolls to use their roads in return for providing roads and maintaining them.[178] However, corruption within these Trusts was rife, and oftentimes money was either misappropriated or not used effectively.[179] The roads were not able to bear heavy loads, and the Industrial Revolution instead saw an expansion of the canal and rail network to transport both goods and people. This lessened demand for travel by road and, as a result, the Turnpikes saw a reduction of monies collected, leading to neglect in road maintenance and the closing of large numbers of the Turnpike Trusts in the late 1800s. As a consequence, the maintenance of roads once again reverted back to local parishes.[180] By 1888, the national roads were in such a state of neglect that Parliament acted and imposed responsibility for the maintenance of roads on the newly created county councils.[181]

The 1909 budget introduced the first tax on all vehicles in England (with rates based on horsepower) and a tax on oil.[182] The Development and Road Improvement Fund Act 1909[183] established a road fund, through which all roads in England were funded. All car taxes that were collected by county councils were paid into this fund, which was then passed along to local authorities to finance road improvements and maintenance. In practice, the fund was "never spent in full and was notorious for being raided for other purposes."[184] It was formally ended in 1936 after Winston Churchill asserted the following:

> [I]t is a monstrous assertion that any important body of taxpayers should claim proprietary rights over the particular quota of taxation which they contribute, and that all should not be brought into an area freely justiciable by the House of Commons.[185]

Since 1937, all monies raised from these taxes have been paid directly into the Consolidated Fund, the government's general bank account held at the Bank of England.[186] The annual budget determines the allocation of these funds.

III. National Road Infrastructure Funding

The Department for Transport is the government department responsible for the provision of roads in England. The maintenance, operation, and improvement of the strategic road network in England, made up of 4,300 miles of motorways and major roads, or "trunk roads" (the most significant 'A' roads),[187] is the responsibility of the Highways Agency,[188] which was created in 1994. The strategic road network comprises less than 2% of roads by length in the United Kingdom but carries the vast majority of traffic.[189] The Highways Agency has a statutory responsibility to maintain these highways;[190] in FY 2012/13, a third of the Highways Agency's budget was devoted solely to maintenance.[191]

The money provided from the government is put forth each year in the annual budget, which allocates annual spending from the Consolidated Fund.[192] The exact amount to be spent on highways is then determined by a Spending Round, a government led "process to allocate resources across all government departments, according to the government's priorities."[193] From 2010/11–2014/15 the government is slated to provide over £1.6 billion (approximately US$2.7 billion) for the maintenance of highways.[194] However, during the most recent Spending Round, the government announced that to provide certainty for the Highways Agency, it will provide long-term funding over time periods of at least five years in length.[195] Accordingly, it has allocated £12 billion (approximately US$19.9 billion) to maintain the local and national highway networks from 2015/16–2020/21. Half of the funds have been allocated to the Highways Agency for the renewal of the strategic road network and half to local authorities for local maintenance and renewal.[196] The Secretary of State for Transport is responsible for the government's policy on strategic roads and determines the financial resources for these roads.[197] Any strategic road project that requires funding of more than £10 million (approximately US$16 million) is generally financed through public funds, or through a private-public partnership.[198]

The maintenance of local roads remains the responsibility of local authorities in each area. The Department for Transportation provides policy, guidance, and funding to local authorities to help them with their road networks. This funding covers operational costs, maintenance, and the development of new major transport schemes.[199] There is no single point of funding for local authorities to spend on roads; instead, road funding is taken from a number of available sources, including government grants, locally charged council taxes, and other fees and charges. The cost of road maintenance in 2011/12 was £1.63 billion (approximately US$2.7 billion).[200]

The government's current focus regarding road infrastructure is on improving the efficiency and effectiveness of existing roads, rather than building new ones. The government has stated that it does not intend to actively seek out private financiers to build new toll roads.[201] Despite this, funding continues for various projects in process, and new funding has been allocated for fourteen new projects that will alleviate congestion and improve roadways.[202]

IV. Transportation Taxes and Duties

A. Vehicle Taxes

England taxes car owners in two ways. The first is a vehicle excise duty (VED), which is charged on every registered "mechanically propelled vehicle" and is a tax on ownership.[203] The second is a fuel duty, a tax on the use of cars. Historically, the monies raised from these taxes were specifically used for building and maintaining roads. In 1937 this changed, and these taxes are now a means of raising "general revenue."[204] Any changes to rates are made in the annual Finance Acts, which implement that the budget the government announces each year.[205]

The current rate of VED for cars is tied to the carbon dioxide emissions of vehicles built after 2001. Since 2001, there has been a first-year tax that is charged at a higher rate than the subsequent annual tax. The rate varies according to the level of carbon dioxide emissions, and ranges from charges of £0 for vehicles that emit less than 100g of CO2 per kilometer up to £1,065 (approximately US$1,700) for vehicles that emit over 255g of CO2 per kilometer. After the first-year tax, the subsequent annual tax ranges from £0 for vehicles that emit less than 100g of CO2 per kilometer up to £490 (approximately US$780) for vehicles that emit over 255g of CO2 per kilometer.[206] For heavy goods vehicles (HGVs) the rate of the annual tax does not vary from year to year and is tied primarily to weight. It ranges from £165 (approximately US$265) to £1,850 (approximately US$3,000). There is a discounted rate for low-polluting HGV's, which ranges from £160 (approximately US$255) to £1,350 (approximately US$2,200).[207] It is an offense to keep a vehicle without paying the VED, unless a statutory off-road license is in effect.[208]

B. Fuel Taxes

The second manner in which England taxes car owners is the fuel duty—a tax on gas, or on the use of a vehicle. The two main fuels used by vehicles in England—ultra-low sulfur petrol and ultra-low sulfur diesel—are charged excise duty at 57.95 pence per liter (approximately US$0.95 per liter, or approximately US$3.59 per gallon).[209] When the value-added tax (charged on almost every good sold in the country) is factored in, taxes make up around 60% of the price paid for gas and diesel fuel in England.[210]

C. Heavy Goods Vehicle Road Levy

England is part of the European Union (EU), which provides for free movement of goods and people within EU countries. England is also physically connected to continental Europe by the Channel Tunnel, while ferries provide an easy connection to France. These factors have led to England's road haulage companies facing competition from European road haulers, who do not pay England's road taxes and can often avoid the high fuel duties by filling up across the Channel before arriving in England. In an attempt to counterbalance the financial burden of taxes and duties faced by road haulers, the government introduced the HGV Road User Levy Act 2013.[211] This Act implements a road levy specific to HGVs, with the aim of ensuring that these vehicles make a contribution for the wear and tear they cause to the road network.[212] The road levy is due to enter into effect in April 2014, and the funds generated will be paid into the Consolidated Fund. Both English and foreign haulers will be required to pay the levy on vehicles weighing more than twelve tons, with a maximum daily charge of €11 (approximately US$15), set in accordance with vehicle excise duty bands.[213] HGVs and foreign HGVs will pay the levy prior to entering the UK. UK HGVs will pay the levy as part of their vehicle excise duty and get a reduced rate on the HGV levy portion of the duty, with the result that the majority of UK-registered operators will not pay more than they do at the moment.[214] There is a penalty of up to £5,000 (approximately US$8,000) for nonpayment of this levy, which is expected to raise £80 million (approximately US$130 million) from 2014–2017/18.[215]

D. Tolls

Despite the historically prolific use of tolls in England, the collection of tolls on modern roads has been very limited.[216] The government has the authority to implement a toll on any road that has received consent for construction under the Planning Act 2008.[217] In 2013, the government looked at using this provision to introduce a toll on a road it was improving that required significant amounts of investment. After hearing concerns from residents and businesses, the government decided against implementing a toll when the road is finally constructed.[218] The charging of tolls by the public sector is regulated by section 167 of the Transport Act 2000.[219] This section provides that a toll may be implemented only on a trunk road that the

Secretary of State has authority for, and that the road must include either a bridge or tunnel that is at least six hundred meters long. The current government published a report in 2013 that looked at future models for roads in England and stated that the use of tolls for new roads remains a possibility, but that it is unwilling to introduce tolls for existing roads.[220] Any revenue generated from tolls goes to the highway authority and must be used for the road network or related transportation measures.[221] Local authorities may introduce tolls on roads, but only if there is a local transport plan in place to achieve such aims as reducing congestion or preventing traffic growth.[222] The London congestion charge (see discussion, Part V(B), below) implemented in 2008 by London's first elected mayor, Ken Livingstone, was introduced under similar provisions as those provided in the Transport Act 2000, but at the time the powers to implement such charges were available only in the Greater London area under the Greater London Authority Act 1999.[223]

Tolls by private companies are regulated by the New Roads and Street Works Act 1991.[224] This Act provides that in return for financing, constructing, building, or maintaining a road, the operator may charge a toll.[225]

V. New Initiatives on Transportation Taxes and Duties

A. "Road-Pricing" Structure

The VED and petrol tax system is the one currently in operation in England and Wales. However, a former Transport Minister has noted that the movement towards cleaner gas-driven and electric cars will force whichever government is in power to change the tax structure towards a "road-pricing" structure. Under this structure, users would pay on a usage basis—those making heavy use of the roads would pay more, and those making smaller journeys would pay less. The Minister stated that

> [i]n the medium term, there's no question that we're going to have to move towards road- pricing and I would like it to be on a revenue neutral basis for the average motorist. So what you pay in using the roads, you get off in road taxes and fuel so that you end up even on it. It wouldn't be an extra tax, it would be just a different way of raising money.[226]

As of yet, no new initiative has been put forward in legislation.

B. London Congestion Charge

The London congestion charge has been in existence since February 2003. It was introduced by a statutory instrument,[227] issued under the powers provided to the Mayor by the Greater London Authority Act 1999.[228] The congestion charge requires users of central London roads to pay a fee each day they drive their vehicle in a specific area during the period of 7:00 a.m.–6:00 p.m., Monday through Friday. The current charges are £9 if paid automatically, £10 if paid on the day of travel, or £12 if paid the following day (these charges range from approximately US$14–20).[229] There are penalties of up to £130 (approximately US$200) if a vehicle enters the congestion charge area and does not pay. There are no toll gates for this area; instead it is monitored by closed-circuit television, and license plate numbers are read and checked against a database to check for payments or exemptions.[230]

The Transport Act 2000[231] provided the power to the Secretary of State to charge other local road users throughout the rest of England and Wales. To encourage the spread of road charging plans by local authorities, the Labor government provided incentives in the form of a £9.5 billion (approximately US$15.2 billion) Transport Innovation Fund, which was available from 2005–10. Very few areas implemented such plans and the fund was dissolved in 2010. The reasons cited for the failure were the lack of public acceptance for charging, and the fund's overly narrow focus in addressing solely the issue of congestion.[232]

FRANCE

Summary

French roads are divided into three main categories: municipal, departmental, and national. The latter category includes both highways and other national roads. Different levels of government have jurisdiction over different types of roads, but the construction of new roads is often financed by more than one source. No special tax or duty is specifically tied to funding road infrastructure, except that many French highways are funded by tolls. Furthermore, these toll highways are managed by private companies under a concession system. A recent effort by the French government to impose tolls on heavy vehicles using national roads and highways that are not under a concession regime was postponed in the face of strong popular opposition.

I. Introduction: Organization of the French Road System

French roads fall into three categories, according to which level of government has authority over them. The national road system (*voirie nationale*) is part of the state's domain,[233] and is itself divided into two subcategories: highways (*autoroutes*) and national roads (*routes nationales*).[234] Departmental roads (*routes départementales*) belong to the *départements*[235] in which they lie.[236] Lastly, local municipal roads (*voies communales*) belong to the municipalities.[237]

There were about 21,157 km of roads in the national road system as of 2011, including 11,412 km of highways and 9,745 km of other national roads.[238] In addition, there were about 377,857 km of departmental roads and 654,201 km of municipal roads.[239]

Although the responsibilities for building and maintaining roads are divided among the three levels of government as mentioned above, the state nevertheless has the duty to ensure the coherence and efficiency of the French road network as a whole.[240]

II. Funding of National Road Infrastructure

The national road system is a "coherent network of roads and highways of national or European interest."[241] The government is supposed to issue a decree every ten years determining which roads belong to the national road system.[242] This national road system is subdivided into two categories: highways and "national roads." All roads belonging to the national road system that are not highways are considered national roads.[243]

A. Construction of New Road Infrastructure

1. National Roads in General

New road projects are managed through one of twenty-one *services régionaux de maîtrise d'ouvrage* (regional construction management services), which ultimately fall under the authority of the Ministry of the Environment, Sustainable Development and Energy.[244]

New road developments can be financed by governmental spending (either by the state on its own, or in partnership with other levels of government, such as regions or départements) or by public-private partnerships.[245] A third approach, consisting of a concession arrangement, may also be used for highways (see part II(A)(*2*), below).[246]

Public-private partnerships allow the state to hire a private company to take charge of one or several aspects of a new infrastructure project, such as financing, planning, construction, maintenance, or management.[247]

The state's financial contribution to any road infrastructure project is undertaken through the Agence de financement des infrastructures de transport de France (AFITF) (Agency for the Funding of the Transportation Infrastructure of France).[248] The AFITF's financial resources are principally made up of the following elements:

- contributions from the state
- fees paid by highway concessionaires
- a special tax paid by highway concessionaires
- 40% of fines resulting from automatic control and penalty systems
- income from investments
- loans[249]

The AFITF also benefitted from a one-time allocation of €4 billion (about US$5.5 billion), which came from the proceeds of the privatization of highway concessionary companies in 2006.[250]

2. Highways and Highways Tolls

Article L122-4 of the French Code of the Road System states that "the use of highways is free in principle." That same article, however, goes on to say that the state may install toll systems to help finance the construction, management, maintenance, and development of that infrastructure.[251] The state may also delegate the construction, management, maintenance, and development of a highway to a third party under a concession system, in which case the toll may also serve as profit for that third party.[252] Furthermore, a highway may be financed jointly by a concessionary, the state, and/or a local government (such as a département), and toll proceeds may then be shared between the partner entities.[253]

A special body called the Caisse nationale des autoroutes (CNA) (National Highway Fund) exists to facilitate the financing of highway construction. Concessionaires may borrow from the CNA for the purposes of constructing and managing highways.[254] The CNA's own financial resources come primarily from issuing bonds on the primary bond market.[255]

As of 2011, approximately 75% of French highways were the objects of a concession.[256]

Toll rates are normally based on the type of vehicle, and the distance between the vehicle's entry and exit points on a particular highway.[257] Thus, in 2013, a car driven on the highway between Toulouse and Bordeaux paid €18.80 (about US$25.70), whereas a tractor-trailer or heavy bus paid €57.20 (about US$78.25) for the same trip.[258] The per-kilometer rates can vary significantly among different routes, as the toll rates for conceded highways are set by the individual concessionaires.[259] Furthermore, additional fees may be charged for the use of certain tunnels.[260]

B. Maintenance of Existing Roads

1. National Roads

The state maintains and manages existing national roads through local agencies called *directions interdépartementales des routes* (interdepartmental directorates for roads), or DIR.[261] These agencies, of which there are currently eleven,[262] and which fall under the authority of the Ministry of the Environment, Sustainable Development and Energy,[263] are tasked with the maintenance and management of the national road system.[264]

The maintenance of national roads is financed by the general national budget, by cofinancing from local authorities (municipal, departmental, or regional governments), and by the AFITF.[265]

2. Highways

Concessionaires are responsible for the maintenance and management of the highways conceded to them.[266] In the case of nonconceded highways, the state is responsible for maintenance and management in the same manner as for other national roads.[267]

In theory, the maintenance of highways can be financed by tolls regardless of whether that highway is the object of a concession or not.[268] In practice, however, only conceded highways currently have tolls.[269] The maintenance of these conceded highways, therefore, is primarily financed by tolls, while the maintenance of nonconceded highways is financed in the same manner as other national roads.[270]

III. Funding of Departmental and Municipal Road Infrastructure

A. Departmental Roads

Each département is responsible for funding the layout, construction, and maintenance of the departmental roads within it.[271] The general councils of the départements are required to include expenditures for the construction and maintenance of the departmental roads in their yearly budgets.[272]

The general councils have fairly extensive budgetary powers, including the ability to incur debts[273] and the power to impose departmental taxes.[274] These may include taxes on motor vehicles,[275] but the proceeds of such taxes are not necessarily tied to expenditures on road infrastructure.

B. Municipal Roads

Each municipality is required to include expenditures for the maintenance of its municipal roads in its yearly budget.[276] Municipalities can generate revenue from various local taxes, or from nontax sources, such as fines and revenue from investments.[277] Spending on municipal roads does not appear to normally be tied to any specific type of revenue.

C. Cross Funding

Construction of municipal and departmental road infrastructure is often financed by more than one entity. Several municipalities can form "public intermunicipal cooperation bodies" (*établissements publics de coopération intercommunale*) to conduct joint projects, including road construction.[278] Other territorial authorities can come together for joint projects as well: a département can participate in a joint project with one or several municipalities, or with regional authorities, or with other départements.[279] Départements can receive contributions from municipalities for investment spending,[280] and each département also receives subsidies from the state for the specific purpose of infrastructure investments (including, but not limited to, roads) in rural areas.[281]

IV. Recent Developments

The French government was planning on implementing a tax on heavy trucks (weighing at least 1.5 metric tons) using national roads and nonconceded highways, starting on January 1, 2014.[282] This tax, commonly referred to as the *écotaxe*, was meant to contribute to the financing of transportation infrastructures.[283] The écotaxe was to be calculated on a per-kilometer basis, based on the vehicle's size and age, and modified according to its level of polluting emissions.[284]

The prospect of paying this écotaxe triggered significant demonstrations, some of them violent, particularly in the region of Brittany.[285] This eventually led the government to postpone the implementation of this tax,[286] perhaps until 2015.[287]

GERMANY

Summary

Germany does not have a national highway fund. Federal highways are funded by the federation through a combination of general revenue and receipts from tolls imposed on truck traffic. The revenues from the German taxes on gasoline and motor vehicle registration accrue to the federation, yet they are not tied to highway maintenance or construction. Plans for requiring passenger cars to pay tolls on federal highways are under discussion.

I. Introduction

Germany differentiates between federal, state, and municipal roads and highways. Federal highways consist of the long-distance interstate highways (*Autobahnen*), major divided four-lane highways that connect to the interstate system, and some thoroughfares through local communities.[288] Most other highways and roads belong to the states, except for the road systems of major municipalities, for which these municipalities are responsible.[289] The federation is responsible for maintaining and constructing federal highways. The states, on the other hand, have the responsibility of administering the federal highways within their territory, a task that they carry out under the supervision of the federation.[290] This administrative responsibility includes setting up and maintaining the agencies that administer federal highway construction and maintenance.[291]

In accordance with the constitutional principle that each governmental body finances the expenditures for which it is responsible,[292] the federation bears the burden of financing the construction and maintenance of federal highways. The states, on the other hand, are responsible for financing the administrative activities that relate to the federal highways and also for all expenditures connected to state highways and roads.

In the German fiscal system, revenue is generated primarily through taxes imposed through federal law. The revenue from some of these taxes is either allocated exclusively to the federation, the states, or the municipalities, or is shared between these entities. In particular, individual and corporate income tax and value-added tax revenues are shared.[293]

II. Funding for National Road Infrastructure

Germany does not have a dedicated fund for building and maintaining highways. The annual federal budget, however, has a highway construction plan that describes ongoing and planned construction projects, and lists the revenues achieved by the federation that are tied to highway construction and maintenance.[294] The most important of the tied revenues is the toll imposed on truck traffic on federal highways;[295] in addition, there is some miscellaneous income, such as fees and concessions. The remainder of the needed funds for federal highway construction and maintenance comes from general revenue.

Germany taxes gasoline consumption within the framework of an energy tax,[296] and the operation of motor vehicles through a motor vehicle tax.[297] The revenue from both these taxes belongs to the federation.[298] In popular opinion, these taxes serve to finance highway construction and maintenance, yet there is no legal requirement for limiting their use to these purposes.[299] Until 2006 gasoline consumption was taxed through a mineral oil tax,[300] and part of the proceeds from this tax were tied to federal highway construction and maintenance.[301] The mineral oil tax was repealed in 2006 with the enactment of the Energy Tax Act,[302] and the revenue from the latter is not tied to highway construction.

III. New Initiatives on Road Infrastructure

Germany has not contemplated alternative means of highway funding, such as a vehicle-miles- traveled (VMT) tax. Instead, there has been an intense debate on the desirability of introducing tolls for passenger cars on federal highways.[303] The most discussed option of the new toll scheme was to impose it only on passenger cars registered in other countries, on the theory that

Germans already pay enough for automobile usage through the taxes on motor vehicles and gasoline. To date, the proposal has stagnated owing to its potential incompatibility with European Union law.[304] The governors of the German states would reportedly welcome the creation of a special highway construction fund to alleviate the current shortage of funding that is particularly felt in the states and municipalities, where many state roads and bridges are in disrepair.[305]

IV. Conclusion

The German experience has shown that the financing of highway construction and maintenance is an urgent task that requires the country to look for new approaches to updating an aging infrastructure. It is not quite clear what lessons can be drawn for the United States from the German experience, considering Germany's geographical situation as a country with considerable transit traffic, the intertwined nature of fiscal and administrative relations between the states and the federation, and Germany's adherence to EU requirements.

ISRAEL

Summary

Funding for road construction and maintenance in Israel derives from both public and private sources. Public funding is utilized for the development of interurban and municipal roads. The state imposes indirect taxes and fees on transportation-related goods and services, including purchase, import, and value-added taxes on vehicles; excise taxes on gasoline; and a variety of vehicle fees such as an annual licensing fees, car radio fee, etc. The construction and maintenance of interurban roads in Israel has been delegated to two government companies, the operations of which are partially funded by private sources. In the case of one of these companies, such sources include the collection of toll- road fees from drivers.

I. Investments in Road Infrastructure

Funding for the development and maintenance of roads in Israel derives from both governmental budget allocations and private sources.

The total governmental budget allocation for roads reportedly amounted to approximately 6.4 billion New Israeli Shekels (NIS) (about $US1.8 billion) in 2013 and NIS 7 billion (about $US2 billion) in 2014.[306] In providing funding for road construction and maintenance, Israel's Ministry of Transportation, National Infrastructure and Road Safety (MTNIRS)[307] differentiates between interurban highways and municipal roads.[308]

This report provides information on funding sources for the development of road infrastructure and maintenance in Israel from both public and private sources.

II. Interurban Construction and Maintenance

Interurban highway construction and maintenance in Israel is conducted by two government companies—Netivei Israel and Cross-Israel Highway (CIH). Funding for the companies' operations derives from MTNIRS allocations as well as from private financing and, in the case of the CIH, also from the payment of tolls by drivers.

A. *Implementation*

1. Netivei Israel Ltd.

Netivei Israel – National Transport Infrastructure Company Ltd. is "a government-owned company that is responsible for the planning, development and maintenance of Israel's interurban road network as well as railway development."[309] According to the Netivei Israel website, the company currently operates a program that is designed to "bring the periphery closer to the center of the country by networking intersecting roads and railways in the north and south."[310]

BdiCoface, an Israeli business information group, describes the operating model of Netivei Israel as one that is "based on outsourced personnel along with salaried employees . . . . [Netivei Israel] regularly monitors, supervises and manages traffic over more than 7,000 km of roads, 1,200 bridges and tunnels and tens of thousands of traffic lights and lighting points."[311]

BdiCoface lists the integration of the private sector in financing, planning, and implementing projects as one of Netivei Israel's main objectives.[312]

2. Cross-Israel Highway Ltd. (CIH)

CIH is the second government company that is involved with the development of road infrastructure in Israel. The company was established in March 1993 with the objective of paving the Cross-Israel Highway. According to information posted on its website, CIH is engaged in promoting the paving of the highway, which extends for approximately 250 kilometers (155.343 miles) from Shlomi in the Galilee to the Negev Junction.[313] The Cross-Israel Highway project is said to be "the first major privately financed project to be implemented in Israel, serving as an important experience for the government, lending institutions and the private sector, and setting the standard for future projects in Israel."[314]

CIH reportedly offered to pave the central section of the highway as a toll road using a concessionaire to finance and pave the road, and to operate it for a period of thirty years. After the expiration of this period, ownership of the highway passes to the state. Accordingly, the Derech Eretz company was selected in an international tender as the implementing authority and the concessionaire of the Cross-Israel Highway on behalf of the state. Derech Eretz is therefore responsible for monitoring the concessionaire's areas of activities that are related to the toll road, including road construction, construction of interchanges, toll gates, cost of travel, methods of collection, road maintenance, etc.[315]

B. Funding Sources

1. Public Funding

The MTNIRS's budget for development of interurban roads for 2013 and 2014 is composed of government appropriations, conditional expenditures, and authorizations to commit.[316] While a conditional expenditure is an authorization for an expense beyond the approved budget expense and depends on receipt of income from nongovernmental sources, an authorization to commit allows the obligation of funds for a plan during the fiscal year, even if payment will be made in the coming years. According to information posted on Israel's Ministry of Finance website, this arrangement allows the government to operate within the framework of multi-year programs while being subject to adequate budgetary supervision.[317] The monetary values of the budget allocation components for interurban road development for 2013 and

2014 were reportedly NIS 5.37 billion (about $US1.52 billion) and NIS 5.9 billion (about $US1.67 billion) respectively in spending appropriations; NIS 17 million (about $US4.84 million) and NIS 18 million (about $US5.12) respectively in conditional expenditures; and NIS 13.2 billion (about $US3.76 billion) and NIS 4.45 billion (about $US1.26 billion) respectively in authorizations to commit.[318]

2. Toll Road Fees

The financing of road maintenance and construction of the Cross-Israel Highway through collection of usage fees is regulated by the Toll Road (Israel National Highway) Law 5755-1995[319] and subsidiary legislation. The Law establishes the rules governing the designation of parts of the Cross-Israel Highway as toll roads,[320] the procedures for selection and replacement[321] of the highway's concessionaire,[322] and the enforcement authorities of the state and the concessionaire.[323]

III. Development of Municipal Roads

Local authorities in Israel are responsible for developing, paving, and maintaining roads, sidewalks, traffic signs, and other transportation equipment located within their jurisdictions. The financing of qualified projects within local jurisdictions, however, is partially funded by MTNIRS appropriations. The Ministry's contributions can be used to develop municipal arteries to ease traffic congestion, increase road safety, and improve road infrastructure in minority communities. Governmental budget allocations for the development of municipal roads during 2013 and 2014 are listed on the MTNIRS website.[324]

IV. Criteria for Taxation of Cars and Gasoline

In addition to toll-road fees,[325] which are collected from drivers based on authorization under the Toll Road (Israel National Highway) Law 5755-1995,[326] the state collects additional revenues that partially support road infrastructure from a variety of indirect taxes. Such revenues go into a general pool rather than a special road infrastructure fund. Indirect taxes on automobile industry products and services generate sizeable revenues for the state.[327] "[I]ndirect taxes are imposed on a citizen's expenses (goods and services) and not on income. Taxes are normally reflected in the price of the commodity/service that the consumer purchased, so that the indirect tax is paid by the final consumer."[328] The following indirect taxes apply to transportation-related expenses:

A. Purchase Tax on Motor Vehicles

A purchase tax[329] is imposed on motor vehicles in accordance with the Purchase Tax (Goods and Services) Law, 5712-1952,[330] as amended, and subsidiary legislation issued under that Law. According to a report published on the Ministry of Finance website,

> [i]n 2011 the statutory purchase tax rate remains as it was in 2010. This after the statutory tax rate reductions beginning in 2005 and the green tax reform starting in August 2009. Compared to the statutory tax rate, the effective tax rate has been in decline since 2000 . . . and in 2011 was about 63%, a fact that can attest to the effectiveness of green taxes.[331]

Lower tax rates were introduced in 2013 for hybrid and electric vehicles to reduce air pollution. It is expected that "by 2020 a uniform tax regime will apply to all vehicle types."[332]

B. Import Tax on Vehicles

Israel applies an import tax on the importation of vehicles. Import tax rates vary depending on whether the vehicle was produced in a country or area that is subject to a free trade agreement (FTA) to which Israel is a party.[333] Current partners to FTAs with Israel include the European Union, United States, European Free Trade Association, Turkey, Mexico, Canada, Jordan, Egypt, Mercosur (the South American-based trade organization), and Colombia.[334] The following rates apply to imported vehicles:[335]

However, specific tax relief rates apply to vehicles according to their air pollution capacity and whether they include safety accessories.[336]

Type of Vehicle	**Vehicles Produces or Imported Directly from FTA Partners**	**Other Vehicles**
Sedan/Motorcycle/Field Car	116%	131%
Collectors Cars	102%	117%
Hybrid Cars (air pollution rates 1-2)	53%	64%
Plug-in Hybrid Cars	42%	51%
Electric Cars	27%	36%

C. Value-Added Tax on Purchase of Vehicles

The value-added tax (VAT) is an additional, indirect tax imposed on the purchase of vehicles.[337]

The current VAT rate is 18%.[338]

D. Excise Tax on Gasoline

Israel imposes an indirect tax on gasoline.[339] The excise tax on gasoline was expected to rise by 1.6% of Israel's consumer price index on September 1, 2013, thereby reaching the rate of 56% of the price of one liter of 95 octane gas.[340]

E. Vehicle Fees

In addition to the indirect taxes listed above, Israel also collects vehicle fees including annual licensing fees, radio fees, transfer of vehicle ownership fees, etc.[341] The total revenues from vehicle fees in 2011 reportedly increased by 0.6% compared to 2010.[342]

ITALY

Summary

Italy's national government provides all funding for national highways, while regions enjoy limited power to fund regional roads. Tax revenue on automobile and gas usage is not applied to dedicated funding for road infrastructure construction. No programs for taxing road usage by vehicle miles traveled exist in the country. Automobile taxes are determined according to several criteria, such as an automobile's environmental impact, engine power, or historical interest. Other factors related to road usage, such as the type of road or road congestion, are not considered in determining automobile taxes.

A percentage of revenue generated by tolls goes to the National Autonomous Roads Corporation (Azienda Nazionale Autonoma delle Strade, ANAS) for monitoring highways under concession.

I. Introduction

According to the Italian Constitution,[343] Italy's national government exercises enumerated powers,[344] but also shares some powers with Italy's twenty regions. These shared powers include passing legislation related to "major transportation and navigation networks."[345] Accordingly, in 2009 Italy introduced the concept of "federal infrastructure" (*Federalismo infrastrutturale*)[246] with the passage of a decree law giving the national government authority to maintain the national highways and limiting the regional branches of the National Autonomous Roads Corporation (Azienda Nazionale Autonoma delle Strade, ANAS) to the maintenance of roads within their regions.[347] After its federalization, the toll system for federal highways and motorways previously managed by ANAS was changed in 2010[348] from a concessionaire-operated toll system to a free- flow collection system.[349]

Appropriations for road infrastructure are stipulated in the annual budget of the national government.[350] The budget law for 2014 includes several provisions related to providing funding for road infrastructure.[351] For example, the Law appropriates €335 million (about US$453.8 million) for 2014 and €150 million (about US$203.2 million) for 2015 to ensure the maintenance of the road network throughout the country, initiation of new projects, and completion of initiatives under program contracts already signed by the Ministry of Infrastructure and Transportation and existing contractors.[352] The same Law also approves funding for the promotion of connections between the sea, rail, and road transportation systems in the area of the Strait of Messina, that is, at the regional level.[353]

Since 2001,[354] the implementation of road infrastructure projects has taken place through the Strategic Infrastructure Program in conjunction with construction projects for the Trans- European Transport Networks (TEN-T) and the Pan-European corridors.[355] Since 2003, the government has sent Parliament an annual report titled *Infrastructure Annex*,[356] in which it informs Parliament about the implementation of strategic infrastructure throughout the country.

II. National Road-Infrastructure Funding

A. Income from Taxes and Tolls

Revenue generated by taxes on road and automobile usage goes to the general Italian treasury. Road usage as expressed through fuel consumption is taxed with an excise tax and a value-added tax (VAT). The excise is a type of consumption tax distinct from the VAT in that it is not proportional to the value but to the quantity of the product.[357] The fuel-consumption VAT, on the other hand, is a general consumption tax that is not tied to road construction or maintenance.

Automobile taxes, in turn, are levied on vehicle owners and are paid independently of car or highway usage. The amount of the tax varies according to the vehicle's engine power. Another factor involved in determining the automobile tax is the class of pollution generated by the vehicle (Euro 1, Euro 2, etc.): the lower the class number, the higher the amount paid because the vehicle pollutes more. Several other criteria also affect the determination of automobile taxes.[358]

With respect to highway-usage tolls under the concession regimen, highway concessionaires have been required to pay an annual fee to the state since 1994.[359] The rate of this fee, which has been modified several times,[360] is currently 2.4% of the net proceeds of the tolls that are due to the concessionaires. Forty-two percent of the fee is paid directly to ANAS, which directs those funds toward supervising and controlling concessionaires in accordance with the relevant costs[361] for maintaining the ANAS network.[362] This is the only exception to the general rule that funds for building roads in Italy are not treated separately from funds for operating and maintaining roads.

B. Other Financing Mechanisms

Other mechanisms for financing public infrastructure projects include "project financing,"[363] the issuance of titles of credit (bond projects),[364] the issuance of bonds by insurance companies,[365] and *defiscalizzazione* (tax exemptions) for certain activities and public-private partnerships (PPPs).[366]

To facilitate the implementation of new infrastructure projects performed through PPP contracts worth a minimum of €500 million (about US$677.4 million), tax credits are granted to holders of PPP contracts via the corporate income tax and the regional tax for activities related to the construction and management of such works.[367]

III. New Initiatives on Road Infrastructure

There are no pending developments in this area. In particular, there are no plans to institute dedicated funds for road construction aside from the general revenue of the state nor are there any plans for taxing road usage by taxing vehicle miles traveled.

IV. Conclusion

It appears that there are no specific funds directed toward financing national highway infrastructure in Italy, which is funded by the general revenue. Highway revenue is generated by taxes and tolls, but this revenue is not tied to highway construction. Likewise, revenues from gas and automobile taxes go to the general revenue of the country, and not to specific highway projects or to the regions.

JAPAN

Summary

Japan traditionally constructed highways through highway public corporations, but these corporations incurred huge amounts of debt over the years. In 2005, four highway public corporations were dissolved and the Japan Expressways Holding and Debt Repayment Agency (JEHDRA) and six new highway companies were established. JEHDRA took over the highway assets and debts of four former highway public corporations and leased highways to the highway companies.

Previously, the major source of government funding for highway construction was earmarked tax revenues, such as the gasoline tax and car-related taxes. The toll from highway users was used to pay off loans. However, the earmarked tax revenue system for road construction was abolished in 2008.

The government supports JEHDRA, and JEHDRA in turn provides financing to highway companies through grants and debt guarantees. The government constructs and manages those highways that are not profitable by themselves.

I. Highway Construction System

Public road planning, including for highways, is under the jurisdiction of the Ministry of Land, Infrastructure and Transportation (MLIT).[368] The

Cabinet determines the routes for "high- standard arterial roads" (highways) in the context of nationwide land planning.[369] The current routes were set in 2008 by the Grand Design of Land in the 21st Century.[370] There are two categories of highways: national expressways and national highways with access control.[371]

A. National Expressways

Routes of national expressways were designated by the Act on Construction of Arterial Roads for Land Development.[372] The MLIT develops the basic plan for a route that is to be constructed upon consultation with the Committee on Construction of Arterial Roads for Land Development,[373] which was established under the jurisdiction of the MLIT.[374] Committee members consist of members of the Diet (Japan's parliament) and scholars.[375] The MLIT then plans the construction upon consultation with the Committee and relevant prefectures.[376]

1. Former Highway Companies

The construction and maintenance of highways may be managed by designated highway corporations.[377] In fact, national expressways were mainly managed by highway public corporations until 2004.[378] In 1956, the first law to establish a highway public corporation was enacted[379] and the Japan Highway Public Corporation (JH) was founded.[380] The toll-road system was introduced in 1952[381] to cover a part of highway maintenance costs and repay construction loans.[382] The JH and three other highway public corporations that were founded later collected tolls from users.[383] In 1970, the Local Road Public Corporation Act was enacted and local road public corporations commenced toll-road management.[384]

There were four main financial sources for national expressway construction: "toll revenues, highway bonds, loans from banks, and government subsidies and social capital fund[s]."[385] However, highway public corporations accumulated huge debts over the years. Those debts and other problems lead to the privatization of these public corporations in the early 2000s.[386] According to experts who analyzed the JH's debt, the two main costs that the JH incurred—the highway construction costs and the corporation's management costs—were financed by three sources: highway bonds, loans from banks, and government investments. The principal and interest for such debts were repaid by toll revenues and government subsidies. Because the JH constructed more highways than its repaying ability could cover, its debts become larger.[387]

In 2002, the Cabinet established the Promotion Committee for the Privatization of the Four Highway-related Public Corporations (Promotion Committee) to examine "new organizational modalities" premised on privatizing JH and other highway public corporations and "ways to ensure [their] economic viability."[388] The Promotion Committee submitted its comments to the Cabinet near the end of 2002.[389] The MLIT discussed the privatization proposal for a year, taking the comments into consideration. Then, the Cabinet made a final decision and submitted bills to the Diet during the 2004 ordinary session.[390] The Diet passed the bills and, as a result of the legislation, four highway public corporations were dissolved and the Japan Expressways Holding and Debt Repayment Agency (JEHDRA) and six highway companies were established in 2005.[391]

JEHDRA, an incorporated administrative organization, took over the highway assets and debts of four former highway public corporations.[392] JEHDRA repays such debts and also pays incremental debts due to new highway construction by collecting highway fees from the six companies. The six highway companies construct and manage highways, and collect tolls. "The lease fees that the companies pay to JEHDRA are variable depending on the level of traffic. The revenue risk is hence transferred from the companies to JEHDRA and ultimately to the Japanese government which is JEHDRA's owner."[393] In addition, JEHDRA holds the interest rate risk when the interest rate of the loans is variable under this system.[394] JEHDRA plans to repay the debts of the former public corporations within forty-five years. After finishing repayment, JEHDRA will be dissolved.[395]

2. Direct Construction by National Government

During the discussion of the privatization of public highway corporations, the Promotion Committee recommended that, "[t]o handle investments for construction that are unprofitable for new companies, the Government . . . establish a new system based on sharing of cost burden with central and local governments under the formula of joint implementation."[396] The government decided that it would directly manage some highways that were difficult to make profitable, but nonetheless important. Such highways have been financed by national and local governments and are free of tolls.[397]

B. National Highways with Access Control

National expressways are a critical part of Japan's national road traffic network. On the other hand, national highways with access control facilitate the smooth flow of traffic, although some of them function almost the same as national expressways.[398] Of the 14,000 km of arterial high- standard highways formulated in the Arterial High-standard Highway Network Plan in 1987, 2,480 km consist of access-controlled national highways,[399] which are managed by the national government.[400]

II. Funding

A. Funding System

JEHDRA borrows money from financial institutions and issues bonds upon the approval of the MLIT.[401] The government may guarantee bonds.[402] JEHDRA also issues Fiscal Investment and Loan Program (FILP) bonds.[403] When JEHDRA provides companies with interest-free loans, those loans are funded by government subsidies.[404]

In the case of national expressways that are directly managed by the MLIT, the national government pays three-quarters of the construction costs, and relevant prefectures pay the remaining one-quarter. Maintenance costs are paid entirely by the national government.[405]

In the case of national highways with access control, the national government pays two-thirds of the construction costs, and relevant prefectures pay the remaining one-third.[406] Again, the national government pays for all maintenance costs.[407]

B. Tolls

The Japanese expressway system consists mostly of toll roads. The system was originally intended to become toll free as soon as the national expressway network was completed and construction debts repaid.[408] However, this did not work as planned.

The highway companies pay JEHDRA the lease fees[409] out of their income from tolls, excluding costs for expressway maintenance and management, and JEHDRA uses these funds to repay debts.[410]

Tolls are expensive in Japan. "Japan's tolls average ¥24.6 per km [about US$0.38 per mile], compared with the equivalent of ¥10.8 to ¥13.45 per km in France and ¥7.01 in Italy,"[411] with the 315.4-km (196-mile) journey from Tokyo to Nagoya on the T□mei Expressway costing 6,900 yen (about US$69) in tolls for an ordinary car. Discounts are available at night and during holidays.[412] With a few exceptions, tolls on national expressways are based on distance traveled.

C. Earmarked (Special Purpose) Taxation

In order to develop the road network, large-scale and stable funding is required. The major source of funding for highway construction in Japan was previously the earmarked tax-revenue system, which appropriated gasoline and car-related taxes.[413] The government established a special fund for financing roads in 1953.[414] After that, fuel taxes and other vehicle-related taxes have been earmarked for road works. The gasoline tax was established in 1954 as an earmarked tax to be sent to the special fund.[415] The following earmarked taxes were then added to the system: a local gasoline tax in 1955,[416] a diesel fuel transaction tax in 1956,[417] a liquefied petroleum gas tax in 1966,[418] an automobile acquisition tax in 1968,[419] and a motor vehicle tonnage tax in 1971.[420] In 1958, the special account for road construction was established, replacing the special fund.[421]

When a manufacturer of gasoline transfers gasoline from the manufacturing location, it must pay gasoline tax. A person who receives imported gasoline from a customs bonded area must also be required to pay gasoline tax.[422] The tax rate is 48,600 yen (about US$486) per one kiloliter.[423] The local gasoline tax is imposed in a similar fashion. The tax rate is 5,200 yen (about US$52) per kiloliter.[424] The diesel fuel transaction tax is imposed on consumers. Manufacturers, importers, or wholesale companies add a tax on the price and pay it to the local government.[425] The tax rate is 15,000 yen (about US$150) per kiloliter.[426] The liquefied petroleum gas tax is imposed on gasoline station operators.[427] The tax rate is 17.5 yen (about US$0.18) per 1 kilogram of liquefied petroleum gas.[428] The gasoline tax and the liquefied petroleum gas tax are considered to fit the benefit principle because the amounts of the taxes are proportional to driving distances.[429]

A prefectural automobile acquisition tax is paid by persons when they acquire a car.[430] The tax rate is 5% of the purchase price for nonbusiness use, and 3% for business use.[431] When the consumption tax is raised from 5% to 8% in April 2014, the tax rate for qualified fuel-efficient cars will be reduced from 5% to 3% for automobiles used for nonbusiness purposes and from 3% to 2% for automobiles used for business.[432] When the consumption tax rate is raised from 8% to 10% (planned in October 2015), this tax will be abolished.[433] A national motor vehicle tonnage tax is paid by vehicle owners at the time of registration and mandatory inspections.[434] In the case of a new passenger car for nonbusiness use, the tax amount is 12,300 yen (about US$123) per 500 kilograms (1,102 pounds). For example, the weight of a Toyota Corolla is about 1,400 kilograms.[435] Therefore, a motor vehicle tonnage tax of 36,900 yen (about US$369) is imposed when the buyer of the new car registers it. In the case of a Lexus LS, which weighs around 2,000 kilograms,[436] the buyer would pay 49,200 yen (about US$492) or 61,500 yen (about US$615), depending on the model. After three years from the date a new car is registered, a vehicle inspection is mandated every two years. Up to the fifth inspection, the owner of a car must pay 8,200 yen (about US$82) per 500 kilograms of the vehicle weight. The tax rate is higher for older cars. The tax is reduced if a car meets ecofriendly standards.[437]

The Japanese government began reviewing this special-purpose tax system in 2005. At the end of 2008, the government decided to abolish the special purpose tax system, and all tax revenues listed above have now been incorporated into the general account as of fiscal year 2009.[438]

MEXICO

I. Introduction

The highway system of Mexico is made up of federal highways, state highways, and rural roads. Federal highways are those that connect with roads from foreign countries; link two or more states of the Federation; and are wholly or mostly built by the Federation with federal funds or through federal grants by individuals, states, or municipalities.[439] Federal highways are built and maintained by the federal government through the Secretariat of Communications and Transportation.[440]

II. Funding for National Road Infrastructure

The Federal Constitution mandates that the states may not in any case "levy duties on persons or goods transiting their territory."[441] In compliance with this mandate, Mexico has networks of federal and state highways that have free access.[442] The federal government finances the construction and maintenance of federal highways with revenues from the annual federal budget.[443] Mexico also has networks of federal and state highways that charge tolls.[444]

Mexico does not tax road usage by vehicle miles traveled (VMT). The Mexican government sets the retail prices of gasoline and diesel fuel monthly. Gasoline and diesel fuel have been subsidized since 2006, whereas previously they were consistently taxed. However, vulnerable groups in society, such as the poor, have generally not benefited from the subsidy because they often lack the income to purchase cars or other goods that use fuel; consequently, since 2010, the government has instituted small, monthly retail-price increases with the aim of eventually phasing out the subsidy. By the end of 2013, these increases had brought Mexican fuel prices nearly on a par with international fuel costs.[445]

The Federal Revenue Law of 2014 mandates that the Special Tax on Production and Services (Impuesto Especial Sobre Producción y Servicios, IEPS) apply to gasoline and diesel fuel,[446] with the aim of reducing the growth rate of greenhouse gas emissions.[447]

III. New Initiatives on Road Infrastructure

Although no official discussion on alternative means of highway funding was located, a recent publication by a Mexican civil engineer on the preservation of federal toll-free highways recommends that funds for highway maintenance be generated through a tax on gasoline.[448]

NETHERLANDS

Summary

The Netherlands funds state highways through a national Infrastructure Fund, which is fed by express lane fees and regular tolls. Provinces, municipalities, and district water boards may also set tolls on motor vehicles passing through certain tollgates on state-managed roads. Additionally, the government applies one-time and recurrent taxes on registered motor vehicles, and levies fuel taxes and a general VAT of 21%. Whether or not these taxes are applied to road construction and maintenance is unclear. In 2009, the Dutch government considered charging a per-kilometer fee for motor vehicle use and abolishing the motor vehicle tax, but that scheme was never implemented. In recent years, the use of public-private partnerships to fund road construction in the Netherlands has enjoyed a revival.

I. Introduction

According to European statistical sources, the highest motorway density in Europe is found in the Netherlands (78 km per 1000 km² on average in 2009), Luxembourg (59), and Belgium (58). As might be expected, the highway network is especially concentrated in the urbanized areas of those regions.[449] In the highly developed highway system of the Netherlands, the costs of infrastructure investment are high "despite the favourably flat landscape" because they "are inflated by high population density, legal and regulatory aspects (*e.g.* complicated and lengthy land-freeing procedures, environmental regulation), a high number of crossings with existing infrastructure and waterways and problems associated with building on wet land, particularly reclaimed from the sea."[450] According to a 2007 study, on average it takes over twenty years from the proposal of a road to its construction, which may reduce the incentive to handle congestion by infrastructure-based solutions.[451]

The main motorways are part of the Dutch national road system (Autosnelwegen).[452] This system is administered by the Rijkswaterstaat (Directorate-General for Public Works and Water Management).[453] The Rijkswaterstaat, which is under the Ministry of Infrastructure and the Environment, "is responsible for the design, construction, management and maintenance of the main infrastructure facilities in the Netherlands," including the main road network, waterway network, and water systems.[454] Roadways are managed by authorities at different levels, including the national, provincial, Water Board (*Waterschappen*), and municipal levels, as well as by ports, individual homeowners, etc.[455]

II. Funding for National Road Infrastructure

A. *Constitutional Provisions*

The Constitution of the Netherlands provides in general that rules on the management of the state's finances[456] and the levying of taxes imposed by the state[457] are to be prescribed by acts of Parliament. Other acts of Parliament are to provide for estimates of the state's revenues and expenditures,[458] regulate taxes that may be levied by the administrative organs of provinces and municipalities, and regulate the financial relationships of those organs with the central government.[459] The regulation and administration of the internal affairs of provinces and municipalities are delegated to their administrative organs, which may be required by or pursuant to an act of Parliament to handle such matters.[460]

B. Road Fees/Tolls

According to the Dutch Law on Accessibility and Mobility, the net proceeds of "mobility rates" (*mobiliteitstarieven*) will be donated to an Infrastructure Fund.[461] Mobility rates are fees payable at the time a motor vehicle with domestic or foreign registration passes through a designated fee payment gateway,[462] at which time the fee is levied on the vehicle owner.[463] Mobility rates are governed by article 15, paragraph 1, and article 21, paragraph 1, of the Law. These paragraphs state, respectively, that a vehicle's express lane fee will be determined by the relevant Ministry and the Minister of Finance to ensure good flow in designated express lanes, and that a "toll" refers to the mobility rate levied by the state on a motor vehicle passing through a designated fee-payment gate on a state-managed road.[464] A province, municipality, or a district water board may likewise set a mobility rate, or "toll," on a motor vehicle passing through a designated gateway on a road managed by the state.[465] For the purposes of the laws on provincial taxation, municipal taxation, and district water board taxation, respectively, this rate is deemed to be a provincial, municipal, or water board tax.[466] Thus, the Netherlands funds road infrastructure not only at the national level but at the local level as well.

The Infrastructure Fund is established under the Infrastructure Fund Act as a fund for the financing and defrayment of the costs of the construction, management, and maintenance and operation of infrastructure that is or will be managed by the government, and for the financing and defrayment of the costs for related basic information.[467] The Infrastructure Fund also finances and defrays the costs of the construction, management, and maintenance and operation of infrastructure that is not or will not be managed by the government.[468]

C. Motor Vehicle Taxes

Motor vehicle taxes are also applied in the Netherlands. Beginning in 2010, the system of using net list-price as the basis for the vehicle sales tax was gradually phased out for passenger cars, and replaced by the vehicle's "absolute" CO_2 emission level as the basis, so that the tax rate increases with the emission level. This has resulted in cheaper rates for fuel-efficient cars and a price hike for those that waste fuel.[469]

Thus, anyone in the country who registers for the first time a car, a vehicle that transports light goods, or a motorcycle must pay a one-time tax called the tax on passenger cars and motorcycles (*belasting op personenauto's en motorrijwielen*, BPM), which is levied on the basis of a car's CO_2 emissions and the van's or motorcycle's list price.[470] The BPM rates are set forth in section 2 (*Tarief*), chapter 3, of the Passenger Car and Motorcycles Tax Act 1992.[471]

The person in whose name a car, van, motorcycle, bus, or vehicle for heavy goods is registered must pay a motor vehicle tax (*motorrijtuigenbelasting*, MRB). This tax, which is to be paid every three months, is based on the registration of the vehicle, not on road use.[472] There is no BPM or MRB payable on electric cars.[473] Chapter 4 of the Motor Vehicle Tax Act 1994 covers the tax rates applicable to various vehicles.[474]

Transport companies must pay a heavy vehicle tax (*belasting zware motorrijtuigen*, BZM, or a Eurovignette), a road-use charge for vehicles that carry heavy loads. Evidence of payment of the tax is valid in the Netherlands, Belgium, Denmark, Luxembourg, and Sweden. For Dutch vehicles the tax is in addition to the MRB.[475]

D. Fuel Tax

The Netherlands applies an excise duty of about €0.846 per liter (about $US1.16) for leaded gasoline and €0.759 per liter (about $US1.04) for unleaded.[476] In addition, there is a value-added tax in the Netherlands of 21%.[477] It is unclear if these taxes are used to fund highway construction, maintenance, and management.

III. New Initiatives on Road Infrastructure

In 2009 the Dutch government considered charging a per-kilometer fee for motor vehicle use and abolishing the motor vehicle tax. That scheme was never instituted, however.[478] The Law on Accessibility and Mobility, while not adopting the road-pricing scheme, was created on the basis of the repealed Road Pricing Act and a package of related measures aimed at improving access to major economic centers in the Netherlands.[479]

The use of public-private partnerships (PPPs) in the Netherlands has revived in recent years and been applied to road construction.

> The Netherlands was one of the first European countries to explore the benefits of PPP. However, after a promising start the Dutch PPP market did not really live up to the expectations. In recent years, however, the Dutch PPP market has been gradually picking up as a result of both the financial crisis [of 2008] . . . as well as the acceptance by many that privately funded projects are beneficial to both public as well as private market parties.[480]

For example, in late August 2012, government officials took "a different approach to helping pension funds meet their goals" by investment in infrastructure projects; specifically, the Ministry of Infrastructure and Environment chose a PPP for a pilot program on expansion and maintenance of highway N33 (a connecting road) for a twenty-year period.[481] However, the government subsequently announced that this would be the only project of its kind.[482] In February 2013, the tender process was completed for a PPP project for the "design, build [sic], financing and maintenance of the extension of the, A1/A6 Diemen-Almere Havendreef" highway" ("A" roads are major thoroughfares).[483]

Another aspect of the roadway infrastructure in the Netherlands is the Intelligent Transport Systems (ITS) initiative. According to a 2012 report published by the Ministry of Infrastructure and the Environment, in conformity with the European Union's ITS Directive (2010/40/EU),[484]

> [t]he Netherlands has invested many billions (in hardware, software, people and expertise) in order to enable the current range of ITS applications. . . . Many millions are also spent each year on operations, management, maintenance and upkeep. For example, Rijkswaterstaat spends around €200 million [about US$2748,648,000] a year on (dynamic) traffic management on the primary road network.[485]

The report noted that in future the country's "Better Utilisation Programme" would invest about €170 million [about US$2482,601,000] in regional-level ITS applications and about €50 million [about US$68,412,000] would be "available for innovative and effective ITS applications at a national level."[486] The report stated, however, that the need to cut costs of road construction, management, and maintenance was resulting in cost cutting for the roadside systems as well, especially ones on the primary road network that provide information to road users.[487]

SOUTH AFRICA

Summary

The South African National Roads Agency SOC Limited (SANRAL), an independent statutory company whose sole shareholder and owner is the South African government, is in charge of all matters affecting the country's national road network. These include the financing, management, control, planning, development, maintenance, and rehabilitation of national roads.

Over 80% of South Africa's national roads are nontoll roads funded largely through government appropriations. The rest are toll roads, over 10% of which are under the direct management of SANRAL, and funded in large part through a mix of toll revenues and capital market borrowings. The latter are generated by auctioning government guaranteed and nonguaranteed bonds. SANRAL has also made limited use of funding for its toll-road projects from additional sources, including direct foreign investment and loans backed by export credit agencies. The remaining toll roads are funded through thirty-year concessions to private investors, who build, manage, and maintain the toll roads for the term of their contract.

I. Introduction

The current South African Constitution established a three-tiered system of government: national, provincial, and local.[488] The national and provincial governments enjoy concurrent legislative jurisdiction over matters relating to public transport and the regulation of road traffic.[489] Provincial governments enjoy exclusive legislative jurisdiction over matters affecting provincial roads and traffic.[490] However, in special circumstances, the national government may legislate on matters exclusively reserved for provincial governments, including those affecting provincial roads and traffic.[491] As a result, there are a number of national and provincial laws regulating roads and road transport in South Africa.[492]

This report briefly describes the legal framework for funding national roads in South Africa. Specifically, it discusses the functions and activities of the South African National Roads Agency Limited (SANRAL), an independent, wholly state-owned statutory company responsible for developing, maintaining, and managing South Africa's national road network, in accordance with its governing legislation, the South African National Roads Agency Limited and National Roads Act.[493]

II. National Roads and SANRAL

A national road is any road or route declared as such; it includes any toll road, interprovincial bridge, and interstate bridge used in conjunction with a national road.[494] The process of having a particular road declared a national road may involve the Minister of Transportation, SANRAL, provincial premiers, and the Constitutional Court. The Minister of Transportation may declare as a national road "any existing road, or any route of which the boundaries have been fixed by survey," and may amend or reverse such declaration.[495] However, the Minister can only do so on the recommendation of SANRAL.[496] In addition, if the road in question is an existing road, the Minister needs to reach into an agreement with the premier of each province in which the road is situated; however, if it is a new road the Minister can declare it a national road upon consultation with the premiers of the provinces that will be affected.[497] If, in the process of having an existing road declared a national road, the Minister and a premier of an affected province cannot reach an agreement, the matter is referred to the Constitutional Court.[498]

SANRAL is in charge of matters affecting every aspect of South Africa's national road system.[499] Incorporated in 1998, SANRAL is an independent statutory company registered in accordance with South Africa's Companies Act, with the South African government as its sole shareholder and owner.[500] It is governed by a board of eight members, most of whom are appointed by the Minister of Transportation.[501] Its main functions include all strategic planning concerning South Africa's national roads; planning, designing, constructing, operating, managing, controlling, maintaining, and rehabilitating all national roads; and financing all these activities.[502]

In addition to its main functions, SANRAL is afforded various additional powers by law. For instance, in addition to its duties regarding national roads, at the request of a municipality or a provincial government and with the approval of the Minister of Transportation, it may perform any of its main functions on roads under the jurisdiction of a municipality or a province on behalf of any such authority.[503] It may charge a fee for any service it provides.[504] It also has the authority to contract out any of its functions to a private person or institution.[505] In addition, with the Minister's approval, it may take part "in ventures, involving national or other roads, jointly with the road authorities, or (as the case may be) any private persons or bodies, who have or will have ownership or control of the other roads."[506] Furthermore, it has the authority to operate any national road as a toll road.[507]

III. Funding of National Roads

The South African National Roads Agency and National Roads Act envisages various sources of funding for SANRAL, including

- capital investments or loans made by the state;
- revenue generated from fuel taxes in accordance with any applicable law;[508]
- loans;
- interest from cash balances or investments;
- revenue generated from participation in joint ventures;
- revenue generated from the sale of assets;
- revenue generated from tolls;
- revenue generated from collecting fines;
- revenue generated from developing, leasing, or managing assets;
- revenue generated from any fees collected;
- parliamentary appropriations; and
- revenue generated from grants, donations, or inheritances.[509]

Currently, SANRAL operates two separate business areas (toll and nontoll operations). The reports on and budgets for each are kept strictly separate for purposes of management and cash flow obligations; "no cross-subsidization between the two are permitted."[510]

A. Nontoll Roads

Most of South Africa's national road network falls into the category of nontoll roads and is largely funded through appropriations. At present, SANRAL manages a road network of 19,705 kilometers (about 151,5144 miles), including both toll and nontoll roads throughout South Africa.[511] Most of these (81%) consist of nontoll roads.[512] The vast majority of the funding for nontoll roads comes from tax-based revenues generated by the national government and disbursed through appropriations; in 510151/51013, this amounted to ZAR9.7 billion (about US$875 million).[513] A small portion of the funding is generated from other income; in the same year this amounted to

ZAR355 million (about US$351 million).[514] Of the total nontoll budget for the year, ZAR466 million (about US$451 million) was allocated for routine road maintenance contracts.[515]

B. Toll Roads

Toll roads are a relatively recent phenomenon in South Africa. Government appropriations were the only source of funding for roads in the country until 1995, when toll roads were introduced to compensate for inadequate government funding for the development, management, and maintenance of national roads.[516] Currently, 19% of South Africa's national road network consists of toll roads.[517] The total budget for toll-road development and management for 2012/20151 was ZAR4.7 billion (about US$424 million), including ZAR2951 million (about US$26 million) allocated for full-time routine road maintenance.[518]

SANRAL is authorized by law to determine which national roads should be turned into toll roads. SANRAL may, with the approval of the Minister of Finance, declare "any specified national road or any specified portion thereof, including any bridge or tunnel on a national road, to be a toll road."[519] However, the Minister determines the amount of the toll that may be imposed as well as any increase or decrease in such fees.[520]

Toll roads in South Africa are developed in one of two ways: SANRAL may fund the development of a toll road and directly collect tolls, or contract the management aspect to a private company.[521] It may also enter into a contract with any person to finance, plan, design, construct, maintain, or rehabilitate a national road and operate it as a toll road.[522]

1. SANRAL-Funded Toll Roads

SANRAL has directly developed and manages about 11% of the over 19,000 kilometers of national roads, which it funds largely through a mix of toll revenues and capital market borrowing.[523] In raising funds for toll roads, SANRAL seeks to follow two key principles: reducing the cost of borrowing and tying the maturity of the funding to the life of the roads.[524]

One of the principal ways SANRAL raises funds to finance toll roads is by issuing government- backed bonds.[525] It has a government guarantee on borrowing of ZAR6 billion (about US$547 million) with no expiration date.[526] This helps SANRAL keep the cost of borrowing low.[527] The country's National Treasury has approved for SANRAL a borrowing ceiling of ZAR527.91 billion (about US$52.3 billion); ZAR37.9 billion (about US$3.52

billion) of this amount will be underwritten by the national government through a guarantee.[528]

SANRAL may also issue nonguaranteed bonds for the purpose of accessing additional sources of funding.[529] It is authorized to raise funds through the issuance of nonguaranteed bonds of up to ZAR15 billion (about US$1.35 billion).[530]

SANRAL bond auctions have been temporarily suspended since September 2011.[531]

In addition to bonds, SANRAL has also explored and made limited use of additional sources to fund its toll-road program. One such source is direct foreign investment. In 2010/2011, SANRAL obtained a government-guaranteed, twenty-year loan from the European Investment Bank in the amount of ZAR1.1 billion (about US$99 million).[532] SANRAL has also explored Export Credit Agency (ECA) supported loans. Recently, SANRAL was able to obtain an Austrian ECA guaranteed line of credit from a local South African bank for ZAR550 billion (about US$539 million) at a favorable rate for the purchase of goods and services to finance a particular toll road.[533]

2. Privately Funded Toll Roads

In addition to the 81% of nontoll roads and about 11% toll roads under SANRAL's direct management, 8% of South Africa's national roads, which are also toll roads, are developed and managed by private parties through concession contracts under public-private partnerships.[534] The concessionaires get a thirty-year term to build the roads, collect tolls, and manage them in accordance with the terms of their contracts; at the conclusion of the concession, they turn the roads over to SANRAL.[535] The roads under concession remain the property of SANRAL, and all improvements made by the private investors are reflected on SANRAL's balance sheet as assets.[536]

SANRAL has awarded concessions to three private companies to build, operate, and maintain three sections of the national road network.[537]

SWEDEN

Summary

Sweden finances its highways through municipal and state taxes. The state receives revenue from the taxation of motor vehicles and fuels, and from congestion fees in the two largest cities. There are two international toll bridges and plans to make part of Sweden's largest divided highway toll-based. Planning for major infrastructure projects is undertaken by the municipalities and the national government. The current national infrastructure plan covers 2014 to 2025.

I. State and Municipal Road Infrastructure Projects

Ownership and responsibility for road infrastructure in Sweden is divided between the state, municipalities, and individuals. Individuals have responsibility for their private roads whereas the state and municipalities have responsibility for public roads. Swedish highways (i.e., divided highways) are all state owned. Because of the division of power between the state and the municipalities, road infrastructure projects are determined collaboratively between state and municipal agencies.[538]

All road construction must be undertaken pursuant to a road plan, which is jointly drafted by Länsstyrelsen (the County Administrative Board), the affected municipalities, and those individuals directly affected by the construction.[539] When the plan affects public transportation, relevant agencies need to be heard as well. In addition to describing the project and its geographic scope, the plan must include a discussion of the proposed project's effects on the environment.[540]

Although municipalities have a responsibility to their own taxpayers, it is possible for a municipality to contribute to the financing of public roads in neighboring municipalities where doing so benefits the municipality, or to the financing of roads owned by the state. However, the contribution cannot be the greater part of the financing.[541] One example of when a municipality might want to invest in neighboring infrastructure is when the municipality attracts a large number of workers (commuters) from the neighboring municipality.[542]

Trafikverket (the Swedish Transportation Administration) is the government agency responsible for state-owned roads. Most highways are state owned. There is no private funding of highways in Sweden; all funding comes from state or municipality coffers, although there are toll bridges (see discussion, Part III, below).

Sweden has developed a National Road Plan for 2014–2025.[543] The Plan allocates a total of SEK 522 billion (approx. US$80 billion) of national budget.[544]

To date Sweden has 98,500 kilometers of state-owned roads and 4,600 kilometer of roads owned by municipalities,[545] in addition to private roads.[546]

II. Taxation of Motor Vehicles

Sweden uses annual taxation of motor vehicles to pay for the costs associated with traffic, i.e. increases in CO2 emissions, wear and tear on road infrastructure, and other state expenses.[547]

The rate of taxation of motor vehicles is dependent on the model year of the car and the amount of CO2 emissions generated.[548] Cars manufactured from 2007 to the present are taxed under the Vägtrafikskattelag (Road Traffic Tax Act).[549] Older cars are taxed at a higher rate under the lag med särskilda bestämmelser om fordonsskatt (Law on Special Provisions Regarding Vehicle Taxation).[550]

For cars manufactured in or after 2007, the tax amount is calculated by multiplying the amount of CO_2 emitted per kilometer during mixed driving.[551] The emission is calculated in grams (above the 55557 g threshold) then multiplied by 20 Swedish kronor (SEK) (approx. US$3.08) per gram of CO_2.[552] The tax is thus based on the gas/mileage emission of CO_2. In addition, a second amount is added onto this calculation if the car uses diesel fuel,[553] effectively at least doubling the tax.[554]

The Swedish government encourages its citizens to purchase or upgrade to newer cars by exempting certain new cars from the vehicle tax for the first five years of a car's life.[555]

III. Fee-Based Financing

Sweden currently has no fee-based system for driving on larger state highways. The state does, however, collect taxes for motor vehicle congestion in Stockholm[556] and Gothenburg,[557] and collects tolls for the use of two international bridges.

A. Congestion Tax

Sweden has adopted the use of a "congestion tax," which is paid more or less as a toll for entering and exiting major cities with a motor vehicle.[558] The tax is paid to the state.[559] Depending on what time of day one enters the city of Stockholm, the tax ranges from SEK 10 to SEK 20 (approx. US$1.54 to 3.08).[560] The government bill proposing the congestion tax said that it was generally being undertaken to either finance infrastructure changes or to influence how the flow of traffic is directed.[561] The tax is meant to shift the preferred means of transportation from cars to public transportation.[562] It is not meant to generate funding to maintain streets but rather to deter the use of cars during certain hours of the day and to pay for the environmental effects of pollution caused by cars.[563] Payment of the tax is made by the individual who is registered as the owner of the car.

There are no physical toll booths for payment of the congestion tax; instead, the license plates of motor vehicles are registered when passing and the owner is then billed monthly by Transportstyrelsen (the Swedish Transport Agency).[564] A missed payment results in an added fee of SEK 500 (approx. US$77).[565]

Sweden first considered implementing a congestion tax in 1989 when a government bill was introduced that would have allowed municipalities to tax entry into their cities after receiving approval from the government.[566] Several government reports and bills were presented without ever resulting in a congestion tax until such a tax was implemented in Stockholm on August 1, 2007.[567]

B. International Toll Bridges

Sweden collects a toll for passage over two international bridges, Öresundsbron (which connects Sweden to Denmark) and Svinesundsförbindelsen (which connects Sweden and Norway).[568] These fees are meant to cover the cost of building and maintaining the bridges. On both bridges the fees are collected through physical and electronic toll stations. At Öresundsbron, Sweden and Denmark divide the toll revenues 50/50.[569] At Svinesundsförbindelsen, Sweden collects tolls from vehicles entering Norway.[570] Motorcycles and mopeds, ambulances, fire trucks, and public buses are exempted from the toll.[571] As of January 2, 2014, it cost SEK 21 (approx. US$57.257) for a car to pass into Norway and SEK 105 (approx. US$16.16) for a truck.[572] Payments made electronically through a form of "easy pass" receive a 157% reduction in the amount of the toll.[573]

IV. Tax on Energy

Sweden taxes oil, petroleum, diesel, etc. in accordance with the Tax on Energy Act.[574] Currently, the tax on petroleum is SEK 5.657 per liter (approx. US$57.11/gallon) and constitutes a subset of the environmental tax, which will increase to SEK 5.85 in 2015.[575] The total national tax is made up of a two-part tax: an energy tax and a CO2 tax.[576] Diesel is taxed at the considerably lower rate of SEK 4.85 (approx. US$0.75) per cubic meter.

In addition, a state value-added tax (VAT) of 25% is added to gasoline and diesel sold to consumers, making the end price of a liter of gasoline SEK14.58 (approx. US$2.24) in 2008 when the actual cost of gasoline prior to taxation was approximately SEK 5 (approx. US$0.77).[577]

V. Future Sources of Financing for Infrastructure Projects

A. E20

Public opinion strongly favors making the two-way highway E20 into a highway without two- way traffic. Such a change would have to be financed partly by the municipalities in the region, as the state has found that the region does not meet the requirements for it to pay the costs of expanding it to a highway with two lanes in each direction (separated by a barrier).[578] Municipal opposition and the state have instead opted for a 2-1 lane option where the highway has a barrier in the middle and alternates one or two lanes in each direction.[579]

B. Förbifart Stockholm

A much debated project, Förbifart Stockholm, that will allow traffic to circumvent Stockholm while traveling on the E4an (a major Swedish highway) may become the first toll road in Sweden, as once built it will be largely financed through user tolls (80%) with the remaining funds coming from the state.[580]

VI. Future Legislation

On December 16, 2013, the government published *Fossilfrihet på väg* (*Fossil Free on the Road*),[581] a report discussing several possible changes to the current calculation of motor vehicle taxes and a possible increase in taxation on diesel of SEK 0.77 (approx. US$0.11) per liter.[582]

The report also proposes a new congestion tax on heavy-duty vehicles based on the kilometers driven.[583]

End Notes

[1] NATIONAL SURFACE TRANSPORTATION INFRASTRUCTURE FINANCING COMMISSION, PAYING OUR WAY: A NEW FRAMEWORK FOR TRANSPORTATION FINANCE 7 (2009), http://finance commission.dot.gov/Documents/NSTIF_Commission_Final_Report_Mar09FNL.pdf.

[2] For a summary of US-based pilot projects on mileage-based user fees, see US GOVERNMENT ACCOUNTABILITY OFFICE, GAO-13-77, HIGHWAY TRUST FUND: PILOT PROGRAM COULD HELP DETERMINE THE VIABILITY OF MILEAGE FEES FOR CERTAIN VEHICLES 61–62 (2012), http://www.gao.gov/assets/660/650863.pdf.

[3] OREGON DEPARTMENT OF TRANSPORTATION, OREGON'S MILEAGE FEE CONCEPT AND ROAD USER PILOT PROGRAM: FINAL REPORT vi (2007), http://www.oregon.gov/ODOT/HWY/RUFPP/docs/RUFPP_finalreport.pdf.

[4] OREGON DEPARTMENT OF TRANSPORTATION, ROAD USAGE CHARGE PILOT PROGRAM: PRELIMINARY FINDINGS 5–6 (2013), http://www.oregon.gov/ODOT/HWY/RUFPP/docs/RUCPilotPrelimFind_Feb13.pdf.

[5] *Road Usage Charge Program*, OREGON.GOV, http://www.oregon.gov/ODOT/HWY/RUFPP/Pages/ruc_overview. aspx (last visited Feb. 3, 2014).

[6] THE CONSTITUTION OF AUSTRALIA, http://www.comlaw.gov.au/Details/C2013Q00005.

[7] THE TREASURY, AUSTRALIA'S FUTURE TAX SYSTEM: ARCHITECTURE OF AUSTRALIA'S TAX AND TRANSFER SYSTEM – SECTION 2: OVERVIEW OF THE TAX-TRANSFER SYSTEM (2008), http://www.taxreview.treasury.gov.au/content/Paper.aspx?doc=html/publications/papers/report/section_2.htm.

[8] AUSTRALIAN BUREAU OF STATISTICS, YEAR BOOK AUSTRALIA, 2012: GOVERNMENT FINANCE – TAXATION REVENUE (May 2012), http://www.abs.gov.au/ausstats/abs@.nsf /Lookup/by%20Subject/1301.0~2012~Main%20Features~Taxation%20revenue~293.

[9] For information on the funding arrangements from a state perspective, see PARLIAMENT OF VICTORIA ROAD SAFETY COMMITTEE, INQUIRY INTO FEDERAL-STATE ROAD FUNDING ARRANGEMENTS (Parliamentary Paper No.361, Session 2006-10, Sept. 2010), http://www.parliament.vic.gov.au/publications/committee-reports/819-final- report-on-the-inquiry-into-federal-state-road-funding-arrangements/download.

[10] *See generally Infrastructure Investment*, DEPARTMENT OF INFRASTRUCTURE AND REGIONAL DEVELOPMENT (DIRD), http://investment.infrastructure.gov.au/index.aspx; *Funding Programs*, DIRD, http://investment. infrastructure.gov.au/funding/ (both last visited Jan. 22, 2014).

[11] *See National Projects: Roads*, DIRD, http://investment.infrastructure.gov.au/funding/projects/roads.aspx; *National Network*, DIRD, http://investment.infrastructure.gov.au/whatis/network/ (both last visited Jan. 22, 2014). The National Network is defined in AusLink (National Land Transport) Act National Land Transport Network Determination 2005 (No. 1) (Cth), http://www.comlaw.gov.au/Details/F2009C00116. This Determination was originally made under the AusLink (National Land Transport) Act 2005 (Cth), which has now been superseded by the Nation Building Program (National Land Transport) Act 2009 (Cth), http://www.comlaw.gov.au/Details/C2009C00304.

[12] *See generally About the Department*, DIRD, http://www.infrastructure.gov.au/department/about/index.aspx (last visited Jan. 22, 2014).

[13] *About Infrastructure Australia*, INFRASTRUCTURE AUSTRALIA, http://www.Infrastructure australia.gov.au/about/ (last visited Jan. 22, 2014). Infrastructure Australia was established by the Infrastructure Australia Act 2008 (Cth), http://www.comlaw.gov.au/Details/C2013C00551.

[14] A New Tax System (Goods and Services Tax) Act 1999 (Cth), http://www.comlaw.gov.au/Details/C2014C00008.

[15] *See About Fuel Prices*, AUSTRALIAN COMPETITION AND CONSUMER COMMISSION, http://www.accc.gov.au/consumers/petrol-diesel-and-lpg/about-fuel-prices (last visited Jan. 22, 2014).

[16] COMMONWEALTH GRANTS COMMISSION, https://www.cgc.gov.au/; *see also Commonwealth Grants Commission*, WESTERN AUSTRALIA DEPARTMENT OF TREASURY, http://www.treasury.wa.gov.au/cms/content.aspx?id=3654 (both last visited Jan. 22, 2014).

[17] The rates are set out in the Schedule to the Excise Tariff Act 1921 (Cth), http://www.comlaw.gov.au/Details/C2013C00555.

[18] For general information on the history of fuel excise in Australia, see THE TREASURY, FUEL TAXATION INQUIRY: HISTORY OF FUEL TAXATION IN AUSTRALIA (Sept. 21, 2001), http://fueltaxinquiry.treasury.gov.au/content/backgnd/002.asp.

[19] The fuel tax credit system is governed by the Fuel Tax Act 2006 (Cth), http://www.comlaw.gov.au/Details/C2013C00594. *See Fuel Tax Credits and Eligible Fuels*, AUSTRALIAN TAXATION OFFICE (ATO), http://www.ato.gov.au/Business/Fuel-schemes/In-detail/Fuel-tax-credits---for-GST-registered-businesses/Calculating-and-record-keeping/Fuel-tax-credit-rates-and-eligible-fuels/ (last modified July 1, 2013); *Frequently Asked Questions Relating to Fuel Tax Credits*, DIRD, http://www.infrastructure.gov.au/roads/environment/fuel_tax_credit/FAQ.aspx (last updated Dec. 4, 2013).

[20] *Fuel Tax Credits – Domestic Electricity Generation and Non-profit Emergency Vehicles or Vessels*, ATO, http://www.ato.gov.au/Business/Fuel-schemes/In-detail/Fuel-tax-credits---if-no-GST-registration- requirement/Overview/Fuel-tax-credits---domestic-electricity-generation-and-non-profit-emergency-vehicles-or- vessels/ (last modified Aug. 22, 2013).

[21] A New Tax System (Luxury Car Tax) Act 1999 (Cth), http://www.comlaw.gov.au/Details/C2013C00099.

[22] *Luxury Car Tax – Getting Started*, ATO, http://www.ato.gov.au/Print-publications/Luxury-car-tax/?page=2#Getting_started (last modified Sept. 3, 2013).

[23] *Luxury Car Tax Rate and Thresholds*, ATO, http://www.ato.gov.au/Rates/Luxury-car-tax-rate-and-thresholds/ (last modified Dec. 17, 2013).

[24] *Heavy Vehicle Charges*, NATIONAL TRANSPORT COMMISSION (NTC), http://www.ntc.gov.au/viewpage. aspx?documentid=2095 (last updated July 25, 2013).

[25] Under the Fuel Tax Act 2006 (Cth), a fuel tax credit is available in relation to heavy diesel vehicles if they satisfy one of four environmental criteria. *Fuel Tax Credit for Heavy Diesel Vehicles*, DIRD, http://www.infrastructure. gov.au/roads/environment/fuel_tax_credit/index.aspx (last updated Oct. 15, 2013); ATO, FUEL TAX CREDITS FOR BUSINESS 13 (2013), http://www.ato.gov.au/uploadedFiles/Content/ITX/downloads/BUS18875n14584.pdf.

[26] National Transport Commission (Model Heavy Vehicle Charges Act) Regulations 2008 (Cth), http://www.comlaw.gov.au/Details/F2008L02216. For information on this legislation, see *Model Heavy Vehicle Charges Act*, NTC, http://www.ntc.gov.au/viewpage.aspx?documentid=849 (last updated Nov. 21, 2013); *see also* DEPARTMENT OF INFRASTRUCTURE, TRANSPORT, REGIONAL DEVELOPMENT AND LOCAL GOVERNMENT, A NATIONAL FRAMEWORK FOR REGULATION, REGISTRATION AND LICENSING OF HEAVY VEHICLES: REGULATORY IMPACT STATEMENT (May 2009), http://www.infrastructure.gov.au/roads/vehicle_regulation/ris/files/HV_RIS_8May2009.pdf.

[27] *Heavy Vehicle Charges – How Are Heavy Vehicle Charges Calculated?*, NTC, http://www.ntc.gov.au/viewpage.aspx?documentid=2311 (last updated June 18, 2013).

[28] NTC, HEAVY VEHICLE ROAD USER CHARGE ANNUAL ADJUSTMENT: CONSULTATION REPORT (Mar. 2013), http://www.ntc.gov.au/filemedia/Reports/HVAnnualAdjustment2013.pdf.

[29] Road User Charge Determination (No. 1) 2013 (Cth), http://www.comlaw.gov.au/Details/F2013L00990.

[30] NTC, HEAVY VEHICLE CHARGES: 2013 ANNUAL ADJUSTMENT TO REGISTRATION CHARGES (Mar. 6, 2013), http://www.ntc.gov.au/filemedia/Reports/2013HVAnnualAdjust.pdf.

[31] *Heavy Vehicle Charges – Heavy Vehicle Charges 2013/14*, NTC, http://www.ntc.gov.au/viewpage. aspx?documentid=2095 (last updated July 25, 2013).

[32] *See generally Heavy Vehicle Registration*, NTC, http://www.ntc.gov.au/viewpage.aspx?AreaId=35& DocumentId=1793 (last updated Feb. 21, 2012)

[33] *About the Project*, HEAVY VEHICLE CHARGING AND INVESTMENT REFORM, http://www.roadreform.gov.au/about- project (last visited Jan. 22, 2014).

[34] Annabel Hepworth, *Trucks May be Tracked by GPS for Fees*, THE AUSTRALIAN (Jan. 15, 2014), http://www.theaustralian.com.au/national-affairs/trucks-may-be-tracked-by-gps-for-fees/story-fn59niix-1226801930220#. The HVCI Reform group's high level proposals were set out in its submission to the Productivity Commission review of infrastructure funding, discussed below in section IV. *See* Heavy Vehicle Charging and Investment Reform, Submission to the Productivity Commission Inquiry into Public Infrastructure (Jan. 2014), http://www.pc.gov.au/ data/assets/pdf_file/0020/131744/sub077-infrastructure.pdf.

[35] *Compulsory Third Party Insurance*, GOVERNMENT OF SOUTH AUSTRALIA, http://www.sa.gov.au/subject/Transport,+travel+and+motoring/Motoring/Vehicles+and+registration/Vehicle+insurance/Compulsory+third+party+insurance (last visited Jan. 22, 2014).

[36] *Registering Motor Vehicles and Motorcycles*, QUEENSLAND DEPARTMENT OF TRANSPORT AND MAIN ROADS, http://www.tmr.qld.gov.au/registration/registering-vehicles/registering-motor-vehicles-and-motorbikes.aspx (last updated Jan. 17, 2014).

[37] *Transport Accident Charge*, VICTORIA TRANSPORT ACCIDENT COMMISSION, http://www.tac.vic.gov.au/about-the- tac/our-organisation/transport-accident-charge (last visited Jan. 22, 2014).

[38] *Vehicle Registration*, NORTHERN TERRITORY DEPARTMENT OF TRANSPORT, http://www.transport.nt.gov.au/mvr/registration (last visited Jan. 22, 2014).

[39] *See generally Stamp Duty – Taxation*, BUSINESS.GOV.AU, http://www.business.gov.au/BusinessTopics/Taxation/ Taxesexplained/Pages/Stampduty.aspx (last visited Jan. 22, 2014).

[40] *Paying Tolls*, NSW ROADS AND MARITIME SERVICES, http://www.rms.nsw.gov.au/usingroads/motorways andtolling/tolling_tolling.html (last updated Dec. 23, 2013).

[41] *Tollways*, VICTORIAN GOVERNMENT, http://www.vic.gov.au/transport-vehicles/roads-road-transport/tollways.html (last visited Jan. 22, 2014).

[42] *Tollways and Tolling*, QUEENSLAND DEPARTMENT OF TRANSPORT AND MAIN ROADS, http://www.tmr.qld.gov.au/Travel-and-transport/Road-and-traffic-info/Toll-roads-and-tolling.aspx (last updated Jan. 9, 2014).

[43] FUEL TAXATION INQUIRY: HISTORY OF FUEL TAXATION IN AUSTRALIA, *supra* note 13.

[44] Australian Land Transport Development Act 1988 (Cth), http://www.comlaw.gov.au/Details/C2008C00377.

[45] FUEL TAXATION INQUIRY: HISTORY OF FUEL TAXATION IN AUSTRALIA, *supra* note 13.

[46] For information on the federal budget process, see *The Commonwealth's Appropriation Framework – An Introduction*, DEPARTMENT OF FINANCE, http://www.finance.gov.au/budget/budget-process/appropriation-bills.html (last visited Jan. 22, 2014).

[47] *See* Richard Webb, Petrol and Diesel Excises (Parliamentary Library Research Paper 6, 2000-01, Oct. 3, 2000), http://www.aph.gov.au/About_Parliament/Parliamentary_Departments/Parliamentary_Library/pubs/rp/rp0001/01RP06. According to an information sheet produced by the Bureau of Infrastructure, Transport and Regional Economics, in the 2008-09 fiscal year the federal government spent AU$4.9 billion on road infrastructure, while state and territory governments spent AU$9.9 billion and local government expenditure was AU$3.4 billion, for a total of AU$15.8 billion. In comparison, a total of AU$15.6 billion was collected in the same year from public road- related taxes and charges. The agency clarified that "[j]oint presentation of the government road-related expenditures with motor vehicle revenues in this information sheet does not imply that there is any direct linkage between revenue and expenditure." DEPARTMENT OF INFRASTRUCTURE AND TRANSPORT, BUREAU OF INFRASTRUCTURE, TRANSPORT AND REGIONAL ECONOMICS, PUBLIC ROAD-

RELATED EXPENDITURE AND REVENUE IN AUSTRALIA 2 (2011), http://www.bitre.gov.au/publications/2011/files/is_040.pdf.

[48] Funding for land transport-related projects is distributed under the Nation Building Program (National Land Transport) Act 2009 (Cth), http://www.comlaw.gov.au/Details/C2009C00304. *See also Nation-building Funds Expenditure Processes*, DEPARTMENT OF FINANCE, http://www.finance.gov.au/investment-funds/nation-building- funds/expenditure-processes.htm (last visited Jan. 22, 2014).

[49] For the various areas of infrastructure funding provided under this system *see* Australian Government, Budget 2013-14, Budget Paper No. 3, Part 2: Payments for Specific Purposes – Infrastructure, http://www.budget. gov.au/2013-14/content/bp3/html/bp3_03_part_2g.htm; *National Partnerships – Infrastructure*, STANDING COUNCIL ON FEDERAL FINANCIAL RELATIONS, http://www.federalfinancialrelations.gov.au/content/npa/infrastructure.aspx (last visited Jan. 22, 2014).

[50] Nation-building Funds Act 2008 (Cth), ch 2 ("Building Australia Fund"), http://www.comlaw.gov.au/Details/C2012C00340. *See also Nation-building Funds: Building Australia Fund*, DEPARTMENT OF FINANCE, http://www.finance.gov.au/investment-funds/NBF/BAF.html (last visited Jan. 22, 2014); *Building Australia Fund Projects*, DIRD, http://www.infrastructure.gov.au/infrastructure/baf/index.aspx (last updated Oct. 17, 2013). For information on the special account appropriation mechanism, see *The Commonwealth's Appropriation Framework – An Introduction*, *supra* note 41.

[51] *Infrastructure Priority List*, INFRASTRUCTURE AUSTRALIA, http://www.infrastructureaustralia.gov.au/priority_list/index.aspx (last updated Dec. 12, 2013).

[52] *Funding Programs*, DIRD, http://investment.infrastructure.gov.au/funding/ (last updated Dec. 20, 2013); *What Is Infrastructure Investment*, DIRD, http://investment.infrastructure.gov.au/whatis/index.aspx (last updated Sept. 18, 2013); DIRD, Budget Statements 2013-2014 – Section 2: Outcomes and Planned Performance, https://www.infrastructure.gov.au/department/statements/2013_2014/budget/dit2b.aspx.

[53] *National Projects*, DIRD, http://investment.infrastructure.gov.au/funding/projects/index.aspx (last updated Sept. 18, 2013).

[54] *Id.*

[55] *Off-Network Projects*, DIRD, http://investment.infrastructure.gov.au/funding/projects/off_network.aspx/ (last updated Sept. 18, 2013).

[56] *Roads to Recovery Programme Funding Allocations 2009-2014*, DIRD, http://investment.infrastructure. gov.au/funding/r2r/index.aspx (last updated Jan. 17, 2014). The original Roads to Recovery program was established by the Roads to Recovery Act 2000 (Cth), http://www.comlaw.gov.au/Details/C2004C01154, which provided a special appropriation over four years. A further four-year program was established under the AusLink (National Land Transport) Act 2005 (Cth), http://www.comlaw.gov.au/Details/C2008C00561, and was funded through annual appropriations. The current program started in 2009 and comes under the National Building program. It is currently scheduled to end in June 2014.

[57] *Roads to Recovery Funding Conditions*, DIRD, http://investment.infrastructure.gov.au/funding/r2r/r2r_funding_conditions.aspx (last updated Jan. 17, 2014).

[58] *Funding for Local Roads*, DIRD, http://investment.infrastructure.gov.au/funding/roads/index.aspx (last updated Jan. 17, 2014).

[59] Nation Building Program (National Land Transport) Act 2009 (Cth): Determination of Conditions Applying to Payments under Part 8 of the Act (Apr. 2013), http://investment.infrastructure.gov.au/publications/administration/pdf/R2R_Funding_Conditions_March_2013.pdf.

[60] *Financial Assistance Grants to Local Government*, DIRD, http://www.regional.gov.au/local/assistance/index.aspx (last updated Oct. 23, 2013).

[61] *Funding for Local Roads*, *supra* note 53.

[62] *Black Spot Programme*, DIRD, http://investment.infrastructure.gov.au/funding/blackspots/index.aspx (last updated Dec. 11, 2013).

[63] *Black Spot Programme Funding Conditions*, DIRD, http://investment.infrastructure.gov.au/funding/blackspots/bs_funding_conditions.aspx (last updated Dec. 11, 2013).

[64] *Black Spot Sites Eligibility*, DIRD, http://investment.infrastructure.gov.au/funding/blackspots/eligibility_of_sites.aspx (last updated Dec. 11, 2013).

[65] Press Release, Liberal Party, Final Update on Federal Coalition Election Policy Commitments (Sept. 5, 2013), http://www.liberal.org.au/latest-news/2013/09/05/final-update-federal-coalition-election-policy-commitments.

[66] Press Release, Hon. Jamie Briggs, Hon. Tony Abbott, & Hon. Joe Hockey, Productivity Commission Inquiry into Infrastructure Costs (Nov. 13, 2013), http://www.minister.infrastructure.gov.au/jb/releases/2013/November/ jb008_2013.aspx. Previously, in 2009, the Productivity Commission published a staff working paper that looked at the financing of public infrastructure from a comparative perspective. Chris Chan et al., *Public Infrastructure Financing: An International Perspective* (Productivity Commission, Mar. 31, 2009), http://www.pc.gov.au/ research/staff-working/public-infrastructure-financing. Later, in 2012, the Infrastructure Finance Working Group, made up of senior officials and consultants, published a report on infrastructure funding reform: INFRASTRUCTURE FINANCE WORKING GROUP, INFRASTRUCTURE FINANCE AND FUNDING REFORM (Apr. 2012), http://www.infra structure.gov.au/infrastructure/iff/files/IFWG_Report.pdf.

[67] PUBLIC INFRASTRUCTURE (Productivity Commission Issues Paper, Nov. 2013), http://www.pc.gov.au/data/assets/pdf_file/0003/130089/infrastructure-issues.pdf. Submissions can be viewed on the Productivity Commission's website, at http://www.pc.gov.au/projects/inquiry/infrastructure/submissions.

[68] *Public Infrastructure*, PRODUCTIVITY COMMISSION, http://www.pc.gov.au/projects/inquiry/infrastructure (last visited Jan. 23, 2014).

[69] Speech, Hon. Warren Truss, IPA Partnerships 2013 – Infrastructure & Investment Conference: Keynote Address (Oct. 18, 2013), http://www.minister.infrastructure.gov.au/wt/speeches/2013/wts005_2013.aspx.

[70] David Crowe, *Drivers Face More Tolls to Use Roads*, THE AUSTRALIAN (Jan. 7, 2014), http://www.theaustralian.com.au/national-affairs/drivers-face-more-tolls-to-use-roads/story-fn59niix-1226796162625#. *See also* Gary Bowditch, *Should Users Pay the Toll for Australia's Infrastructure Problem?*, THE CONVERSATION (Dec. 3, 2013), https://theconversation.com/should-users-pay-the-toll-for-australias-infrastructure-problem-20774.

[71] *National Public Private Partnership Policy and Guidelines*, INFRASTRUCTURE AUSTRALIA, http://www.infrastructureaustralia.gov.au/public_private/ppp_policy_guidelines.aspx (last updated Aug. 21, 2013).

[72] GHD, REVISED FINAL REPORT TO THE DEPARTMENT OF INFRASTRUCTURE AND TRANSPORT: AN INVESTIGATION OF THE CAUSES OF OVER-OPTIMISTIC PATRONAGE FORECASTS FOR SELECTED TOLL ROAD PROJECTS 1 (Dec. 8, 2011), http://www.infrastructure.gov.au/infrastructure/infrastructure_reforms/files/Attach_C-GHD_Report.pdf.

[73] DEPARTMENT OF INFRASTRUCTURE AND TRANSPORT, ADDRESSING ISSUES IN PATRONAGE FORECASTING FOR PPP/TOLL ROADS: CONSULTATION PAPER (Feb. 2012), http://www.infrastructure.gov.au/infrastructure/public_consultations/files/patronage_consultation_paper.pdf; DEPARTMENT OF INFRASTRUCTURE AND TRANSPORT, DISINCENTIVISING OVERBIDDING FOR TOLL ROAD CONCESSIONS (Sept. 2012), http://www.infrastructure.gov.au/infrastructure/infrastructure_reforms/files/Disincentivising_Overbidding_Toll_Road_Concessions.pdf.

[74] *Australia's Queensland State Mulls Sale of Toll Road Assets*, REUTERS (Nov. 8, 2013), http://www.reuters.com/article/2013/11/08/australia-infrastructure-idUSL3N0IT2IT20131108.

[75] Michaela Whitbourn, *Private Funding Dumped in New Plan for Toll Roads*, FINANCIAL REVIEW (June 18, 2013), http://www.afr.com/p/national/private_funding_dumped_in_new_plan_epZkG1r0xOmzcVVKuFvtQN.

[76] Damon Kitney, *Qld Motoways a Likely Target as $63bn China Merchants Group Eyes Investment*, THE AUSTRALIAN (Jan. 20, 2014), http://www.theaustralian.com.au/business/

economics/qld-motorways-a-likely-target-as-63bn-china-merchants-group-eyes-investment/story-e6frg926-1226805393662#.

77 Heavy Vehicle Charging and Investment Reform, *supra* note 29, at 14.

78 *Id.* at 7; Press Release, Council of Australian Governments, COAG Meeting, 13 December 2013, https://www.coag.gov.au/node/516.

79 Lei No. 12.379, de 6 de Janeiro de 2011, art. 1, http://www.planalto.gov.br/ccivil_03/_Ato2011-2014/2011/Lei/L12379.htm.

80 CONSTITUIÇÃO FEDERAL [C.F.], art. 21(XII) & (XXI), http://www.planalto.gov.br/ccivil_03/constituicao/constituicao.htm.

81 The SNV consists of the physical and operational infrastructure of the various modes of transportation of people and goods, under the jurisdiction of the different entities of the Federation. Lei No. 12.379 art. 2. As to jurisdiction, the SNV consists of the Federal System of Transportation (Sistema Federal de Viação, SFV) and the transportation systems of the states, the Federal District, and the municipalities. *Id.* art. 2(§ 1).

82 *Id.* art. 3.

83 *Id.* art. 5.

84 *Id.* art. 6.

85 *Id.* art. 6(II).

86 *Id.* art. 6(III). Lei No. 11.079, de 30 de Dezembro de 2004 [Law No. 11,079 of December 30, 2004], regulates public- private partnerships (PPP). Article 2 of the Law defines a PPP as an administrative concession contract, which can be sponsored or administrative. Paragraph 1 defines sponsored concessions, and paragraph 2 defines administrative concessions. Lei No. 11.079, de Dezembro de 2004, http://www.planalto.gov.br/ccivil_03/_ato2004-2006/2004/lei/l11079.htm.

87 *Id.* art. 7.

88 C.F. art. 150(V).

89 Decreto-Lei No. 791, de 27 de Agosto de 1969, art. 7, http://www.planalto.gov.br/ ccivil_03/Decreto-Lei/1965-1988/Del0791.htm.

90 Article 175 of the Constitution determines that the rendering of public services is incumbent upon the government (*Poder Público*) directly or under a regime of concession or permission, and always through a bidding process. C.F. art. 175.

91 Lei No. 8.987, de 13 de Fevereiro de 1995, art. 1, http://www.planalto.gov.br/ccivil_03/leis/l8987cons.htm. Law No. 8,987 defines "concession of public services" as the delegation of the concession's performance through competitive bidding to the legal entity or consortium of companies that demonstrate the capacity to perform the services, at their own risk and for a specified period of time (art. 2(II)); "concession of public services preceded by the execution of public works" is defined as the construction (total or partial), conservation, renovation, expansion, or improvement of any works of public interest, that are delegated through competitive bidding to the legal entity or consortium of companies that demonstrate the capacity for their implementation, at their own risk, so that the investment of the concessionaire is paid and amortized through the exploitation of the work or service for a specified period of time (art. 2(III)); "permission for public service" (*permissão de serviço público*) is defined as the temporary granting, through competitive bidding, of permission to render a public service, to the persons or entity that demonstrates the ability to perform the service, at their own risk (art. 2(IV)).

92 Lei No. 9.277, de 10 de Maio de 1996, art. 1, http://www.planalto.gov.br/ccivil_03/ leis/L9277.htm.

93 *Id.* art. 3.

94 *Id.* art. 3(§ 1).

95 *Id.* art. 3(§ 2).

96 *Id.* art. 5.

97 Lei No. 10.233, de 5 de Junho de 2001, arts. 1(V), 79–80, http://www.planalto.gov.br/ccivil_03/Leis/LEIS_2001/L10233.htm.

[98] Lei No. 10.336, de 19 de Dezembro de 2001, art. 1, http://www.planalto.gov.br/ccivil_03/leis/leis_2001/L10336.htm.

[99] *Id.* art. 1(§ 1)(I)–(III).

[100] C.F. arts. 159(III) & 177(§ 4). C.F. article 177(§ 4)(II)(c) establishes that the law that creates the CIDE must determine that the funds raised be used to finance programs of transportation infrastructure. Lei No. 10.336 art. 1-A.

[101] For the purposes of article 3 of Law No. 10,336, in accordance with the standards established by ANP, the petroleum-derived liquid hydrocarbons and liquid hydrocarbons derived from natural gas for use in mechanical mixing for the production of gasoline or diesel are considered chains. *Id.* art. 3(§ 1).

[102] *Id.* art. 3.

[103] *Id.* art. 5.

[104] Lei No. 10.636, de 30 de Dezembro de 2002, art. 1, http://www.planalto.gov.br/ccivil_03/ leis/2002/l10636.htm.

[105] *Id.* art. 6.

[106] *Id.* art. 10.

[107] *Id.* art. 11(§ 1).

[108] *Id.* art. 12.

[109] Constitution Act, 1867, 30 & 31 Vict., c. 3, § 92, http://www.canlii.org/en/ca/const/const1867. html.

[110] *Highways*, TRANSPORT CANADA, http://www.tc.gc.ca/eng/policy/acg-acgd-menu-highways-2141.htm (last updated Jan. 4, 2010).

[111] Allison Padova, Library of Parliament, Economics Division, Federal Participation in Highway Construction and Policy in Canada (Feb. 2006), PRB 05-69E, http://www.parl.gc.ca/content/lop/researchpublications/prb0569-e.htm.

[112] *Id.*

[113] *Id.*

[114] *Building Canada Plan*, INFRASTRUCTURE CANADA, http://www.infrastructure.gc.ca/prog/bcp-pcc-eng.html (last updated Oct. 26, 2011). The current exchange rate is Can$1 to US$0.90. *Daily Currency Coverter*, BANK OF CANADA, http://www.bankofcanada.ca/rates/exchange/daily-converter/. For purposes of this report, all references to "dollars" are to Canadian dollars unless otherwise specified.

[115] *Gas Tax Fund*, INFRASTRUCTURE CANADA, http://www.infrastructure.gc.ca/prog/gtf-fte-eng.html (last updated Nov. 22, 2013). Also according to the Infrastructure Canada website, "[t]he federal Gas Tax Fund represents a $13 billion investment from 2005 to 2014. On April 1, 2009, Gas Tax Fund payments doubled to $2 billion annually. Agreements for this funding are in place until 2014. In 2011, legislation was passed to make the Gas Tax Fund permanent at $2 billion per year. Municipalities across the country will continue to receive stable, annual funding for their long-term infrastructure priorities." *Id.*

[116] CAMILA VAMMALLE, OECD, PUBLIC INVESTMENT ACROSS LEVELS OF GOVERNMENT: THE CASE OF BRITISH COLUMBIA, CANADA 11 (2012), https://www1.oecd.org/gov/regional-policy/British%20Columbia_edited.pdf.

[117] *Id.*

[118] *Building Canada Fund*, INFRASTRUCTURE CANADA, http://www.infrastructure.gc.ca/prog/bcf-fcc-eng.html (last updated Oct. 26, 2011).

[119] *Id.*

[120] *Building Canada Fund - Funding Categories,* INFRASTRUCTURE CANADA, http://www.infrastructure.gc.ca/prog/bcf-fcc-categ-eng.html.

[121] *Id.*

[122] *Provincial-Territorial Base Fund*, INFRASTRUCTURE CANADA, http://www. infrastructure.gc.ca/prog/ptbase- finbasept-eng.html (last updated Oct. 26, 2011).

[123] *Id.*

[124] *Id.*

[125] *Canada Strategic Infrastructure Fund (CSIF)*, CANADA-MANITOBA INFRASTRUCTURE SECRETARIAT http://www.infrastructure.mb.ca/csif.html.

[126] *Other Programs*, INFRASTRUCTURE CANADA, http://www.infrastructure.gc.ca/prog/other-autres-eng.html#csif-fcis (last updated Oct. 26, 2011).

[127] *Id.*

[128] *Id.*

[129] *Canada Strategic Infrastructure Fund*, TREASURY BOARD OF CANADA SECRETARIAT, http://www.tbs- sct.gc.ca/hidb-bdih/initiative-eng.aspx?Hi=53 (last updated June 14, 2013).

[130] Canada Strategic Infrastructure Fund Act 2002, S.C., c. 9, http://laws-lois.justice.gc.ca/eng/acts/C-10.3/FullText.html.

[131] *Other Programs*, *supra* note 18.

[132] Public Highways Act, *R.S., c. 371,* § 9(1), http://nslegislature.ca/legc/statutes/pubhighw.htm.

[133] *Majority of Ontario Road Infrastructure Costs Paid by Motorists*, CONFERENCE BOARD OF CANADA (Oct. 17, 2013), http://www.conferenceboard.ca/press/newsrelease/13-10-17/majority_of_ontario_road_infra structure_costs_paid_by_motorists.aspx.

[134] Jeff Nagel, *Road Pricing Viable but Tricky in Metro Vancouver: Experts*, ABBOTSFORD NEWS (Oct. 18, 2012), http://www.abbynews.com/news/174802561.html?mobile=true.

[135] Robert Mackenzie, *11 Ways to Pay for Transit? Metrolinx Proposes Taxes, Tolls and Fees*, TRANSIT TORONTO (Apr. 23, 2013), http://transit.toronto.on.ca/archives/weblog/2013/04/23-11_ways_to.shtml.

[136] CHARLES LAMMAM ET AL., FRASER INSTITUTE, USING PUBLIC-PRIVATE PARTNERSHIPS TO IMPROVE TRANSPORTATION INFRASTRUCTURE IN CANADA 43 (Studies in Economic Prosperity, May 2013), http://www.p3canada.ca/_files/file/Information%20and%20Resources/using-public-private-partnerships-to- improve-transportation-infrastructure-in-canada.pdf.

[137] *Id.*

[138] CONFERENCE BOARD OF CANADA, DISPELLING THE MYTHS: A PAN-CANADIAN ASSESSMENT OF PUBLIC-PRIVATE PARTNERSHIPS FOR INFRASTRUCTURE INVESTMENTS 6 (Jan. 2010), http://www.pwfinance.net/document/research_ reports/12% 20pan%20canadian.pdf.

[139] *History*, 407 ETR, http://www.407etr.com/about/background-information1.html (last visited Feb. 4, 2014).

[140] *Corporate Profile*, PPP CANADA, http://www.p3canada.ca/about-ppp-canada-overview.php (last visited Feb. 4, 2014).

[141] *Id.*

[142] *Overview*, P3 CANADA FUND, http://www.p3canada.ca/p3-canada-fund-overview.php (last visited Feb. 4, 2014).

[143] 中华人民共和国公路法[Highway Law of the People's Republic of China], art. 21, 2004 LAWS OF THE PEOPLE'S REPUBLIC OF CHINA 173–92.

[144] *Id.*

[145] *Id.* art. 59.

[146] ASIAN DEVELOPMENT BANK, FINANCING ROAD CONSTRUCTION AND MAINTENANCE AFTER THE FUEL TAX REFORM (hereinafter ADB REPORT) at 1 (2012), http://www.adb.org/publications/financing-road-construction-and- maintenance-after-fuel-tax-reform.

[147] *2012年公路水路交通运输行业发展统计公报[2012 Highway and Waterway Transportation Industry Statistical Bulletin*] (Apr. 25, 2013), http://www.moc.gov.cn/zhuzhan/zhengwugonggao/jiaotongbu/guihuatongji/201304/t20130426_1403039.html.

[148] 公路养路费征收管理规定 [Provisions on the Administration of Collection of Road Maintenance Fee] (Jiao Gong Zi [1991] No. 714, Oct. 10, 1991) art. 2, WESTLAWCHINA.

[149] 国务院关于实施成品油价格和税费改革的通知[Notice of the State Council on Implementing the Oil Product Price and Tax Reform] (Guo Fa [2008] No. 37, Dec. 18, 2008) (hereinafter Fuel Tax Reform Plan), http://www.gov.cn/xxgk/pub/ govpublic/mrlm/200812/t20081219_33048.html.

[150] 收费公路管理条例[Regulations on Administration of Toll Roads] (published by the State Council on Sept. 13, 2004, effective Nov. 1, 2004), art. 10, http://www.gov.cn/zwgk/2005-05/23/content_241.htm.

[151] Highway Law, *supra* note 1, art. 14.

[152] *2013*年全国公共财政收入12.9万亿元完成全年预算略有超收[*2013 National Public Revenue 12.9 Trillion, Slightly Over Annual Budget*], XINHUANET (Jan. 23, 2014), http://news.xinhuanet.com/fortune/2014-01/23/c_119101065.htm.

[153] 车辆购置附加费征收办法[Measures for the Imposition of Surcharges for Purchases of Motor Vehicles] (issued by the State Council on Apr. 2, 1985, effective May 1, 1985, abolished Oct. 6, 2001), WESTLAWCHINA.

[154] 中华人民共和国车辆购置税暂行条例[Interim Regulations of the People's Republic of China on Vehicle Purchase Tax] (issued by the State Council on Oct. 22, 2000, effective Jan. 1, 2001) (hereinafter VPT Regulations), art. 3, http://www.gov.cn/banshi/2005-08/19/content_24868.htm.

[155] *Id.* arts. 4 & 5. In January 2009, the VPT rate was reduced from 10% to 5% for certain passenger cars to encourage car sales as part of the economic stimulus package while incentivizing energy savings and achieving emission reductions. The rate was then adjusted to 7.5% in early 2010 but reverted to 10% in 2011 for all vehicles. ADB REPORT, *supra* note 4, at 1.

[156] VPT Regulations arts 13 & 14.

[157] *Id.* art. 8.

[158] 车辆购置税用于交通运输重点项目专项资金管理暂行办法[Interim Measures on Special Funds for Funding Key Transportation Projects with Vehicle Purchase Tax] (Cai Jian [2011] No. 93, Mar. 28, 2011), art. 2, http://www.moc.gov.cn/zizhan/siju/caiwusi/zhengceguiding/guizhangzhidu/201302/t20130227_1372317.html.

[159] *Id.* art. 3.

[160] ADB REPORT, *supra* note 4, at 9.

[161] 公路养路费征收管理规定[Provisions on the Administration of Collection of Road Maintenance Fee] (Jiao Gong Zi [1991] No. 714, Oct. 10, 1991), WESTLAWCHINA.

[162] Fuel Tax Reform Plan, *supra* note 7.

[163] 交通和车辆税费改革实施方案[Plan of Implementing Transportation and Vehicle Taxes/Fees Reform] (Guo Fa [2000] No. 34, Sept. 4, 2000), http://www.gov.cn/gongbao/content/2001/ content_60855.htm.

[164] Fuel Tax Reform Plan, *supra* note 7.

[165] *Id.*

[166] 关于提高成品油消费税税率的通知[Notice of the Ministry of Finance and State Administration of Taxation on Raising Oil Product Consumption Tax] (Cai Shui [2008] No. 167, issued Dec. 19, 2008, effective Jan. 1, 2009), http://www.chinatax.gov.cn/n8136506/n8136593/n8137537/n8138502/8734242.html.

[167] ADB REPORT, *supra* note 4, at 20.

[168] Fuel Tax Reform Plan, *supra* note 7.

[169] *Id.*

[170] Chinese highways are classified as Expressways, Class I Highways, Class II Highways, Class III Highways, and Class IV Highways in terms of technical grading. Highway Law, *supra* note 1, art. 6.

[171] Fuel Tax Reform Plan, *supra* note 7.

[172] DAVID BAYLISS, WHAT WENT WRONG? BRITISH HIGHWAY DEVELOPMENT BEFORE MOTORWAYS 4 (Mar. 2008), http://www.racfoundation.org/assets/rac_foundation/content/downloadables/roads%20and%20reality%20-%20bayliss%20-%20highways%20development%20-%20070308%20-%20background%20paper%201.pdf.

[173] Highways Act, 1555, 2 & 3 Ph. & Mary, c. 8.

[174] BAYLISS, *supra* note 1.
[175] *Id.*
[176] 1 WILLIAM T. JACKMAN, THE DEVELOPMENT OF TRANSPORTATION IN MODERN ENGLAND 242 (Cambridge University Press 1917).
[177] BAYLISS, *supra* note 1, at 5.
[178] *Id.*
[179] JACKMAN, *supra* note 5.
[180] BAYLISS, *supra* note 1, at 5.
[181] Local Government Act 1888, 51 & 52 Vict., c. 51, § 11, http://www.legislation.gov. uk/ukpga/Vict/51-52/41/contents.
[182] 4 PARL. DEB., H.C. (5th ser.) (1908–09), 495–98 and 502–05, *available at* http://hansard.millbanksystems.com/sittings/1909/apr/29.
[183] Development and Road Improvement Fund Act 1909, Edw. 7, c. 47. *See also* 24 THE LAWS OF ENGLAND (Rt. Hon. Earl of Halsbury et al. eds., 1912).
[184] LOUISE BUTCHER, ROADS: VEHICLE EXCISE DUTY (VED), HOUSE OF COMMONS LIBRARY STANDARD NOTE, Jan.17, 2013, H.C. SN01482, at 4, http://www.parliament.uk/briefing-papers/SN01482.pdf.
[185] 311 PARL. DEB., H.C. (5th ser.) (1935–36) 327, *available at* http://hansard.millbanksystems. com/commons/1936/apr/23/amendment-of-law.
[186] *Consolidated Fund*, WWW.PARLIAMENT.UK, www.parliament.uk/site-information/glossary/consolidated-fund/ (last visited Jan. 14, 2014).
[187] *What We Do*, HIGHWAYS AGENCY, http://www.highways.gov.uk/about-us/what-we-do/ (last visited Jan. 13, 2014). A map of the roads that the Highways Agency is responsible for is available at http://www.highways.gov.uk/wp-content/uploads/2012/07/Highways_Agency_Network_Map_-_November_2011.gif?9d7bd4 (last visited Jan. 13, 2014).
[188] *Id.*
[189] *Id.*
[190] Highways Act 1980, c. 66, § 41, www.legislation.gov.uk/ukpga/1980/66/contents.
[191] LOUISE BUTCHER, ROADS: MAINTENANCE, REPAIRS AND STREET WORKS, HOUSE OF COMMONS LIBRARY STANDARD NOTE, Aug. 5, 2013, H.C. SN739, at 3, http://www.parliament.uk/briefing-papers/SN00739.pdf.
[192] HER MAJESTY'S TREASURY, BUDGET 2013, (2012–13), HC 1033, www.gov.uk/government/uploads/system/uploads/attachment_data/file/221885/budget2013_complete.pdf.
[193] HM Treasury, *What is the Spending Round?*, GOV.UK (June 14, 2013), www.gov.uk/government/news/what-is- the-spending-round.
[194] BUTCHER, *supra* note 20, at 6.
[195] DEPARTMENT FOR TRANSPORT, ACTION FOR ROADS: A NETWORK FOR THE 21ST CENTURY 4.9 (July 2013), www.gov.uk/government/uploads/system/uploads/attachment_data/file/212590/action-for-roads.pdf.
[196] DEPARTMENT FOR TRANSPORT, GEARING UP FOR EFFICIENT HIGHWAY DELIVERY AND FUNDING (Jan. 2014), https://www.gov.uk/government/uploads/system/uploads/attachment_data/file/273820/efficient-funding-2015-2021.pdf.
[197] LOUISE BUTCHER, ROADS: HIGHWAY INFRASTRUCTURE, HOUSE OF COMMONS LIBRARY STANDARD NOTE, Nov. 2, 2010, SN/BT/1448, at 2, http://www.parliament.uk/briefing-papers/ SN01448.pdf.
[198] *Highways Agency's Major Road Schemes Programme*, HIGHWAYS AGENCY, www.highways.gov.uk/our-road-network/managing-our-roads/improving-our-network/major-projects/highways-agencys-future-delivery- programmes/ (last visited Jan. 14, 2014). *See also Private Finance Initiatives – Design Build Finance and Operate (DBFO)*, HIGHWAYS AGENCY, www.highways.gov.uk/our-road-network/managing-our-roads/operating-our- network/how-we-manage-our-roads/private-finance-initiatives-design-build-finance-and-operate-dbfo/ (last visited Jan. 14, 2014).

[199] *What We Do*, DEPARTMENT FOR TRANSPORT, https://www.gov.uk/government/ organisations/ department-for- transport/about (last visited Jan. 13, 2014).

[200] BUTCHER, *supra* note 20, at 3.

[201] TRANSPORT COMMITTEE, UNCORRECTED TRANSCRIPT OF ORAL EVIDENCE: THE SECRETARY OF STATE'S PRIORITIES FOR TRANSPORT, July 2010, HC 359, at 26, http://www. publications.parliament.uk/pa/cm201011/cmselect/cmtran/uc359/uc35901.htm.

[202] BUTCHER, *supra* note 20, at 3.

[203] Vehicle Excise and Registration Act, 1994, c.22, § 1, www.legislation.gov.uk /ukpga/1994/22/contents.

[204] BUTCHER, *supra* note 13, at 1.

[205] *Id.*

[206] DRIVER & VEHICLE LICENSING AGENCY, RATES OF VEHICLE TAX, V149 (2013), www.gov.uk/government/uploads/system/uploads/attachment_data/file/175492/V149_rates _of_vehicle_tax.pdf.

[207] *Id.*

[208] Vehicle Excise and Registration Act, 1994, c.22, § 29, www.legislation.gov.uk/ukpga/ 1994/22/contents.

[209] *Fuel Duty*, HM REVENUE AND CUSTOMS, https://www.gov.uk/fuel-duty (last updated Sept. 26, 2012).

[210] ANTONY SEELY, TAXATION OF ROAD FUELS, HOUSE OF COMMONS LIBRARY STANDARD NOTE, Jan. 10, 2014, SN824, http://www.parliament.uk/briefing-papers/SN00824.pdf.

[211] HGV Road User Levy Act, 2013, c. 7, http://www.legislation.gov.uk/ukpga/2013/7/contents.

[212] *HGV Road User Levy*, DEPARTMENT FOR TRANSPORT (Sept. 26, 2013), www.gov.uk/ government/collections/hgv- road-user-levy.

[213] LOUISE BUTCHER, ROADS: LORRY ROAD USER CHARGING, HOUSE OF COMMONS LIBRARY STANDARD NOTE, Apr.17, 2013, SN588, at 2, http://www.parliament.uk/briefing-papers/ SN00588.pdf.

[214] *HGV Road User Levy*, *supra* note 41.

[215] BUTCHER, *supra* note 42, at 2.

[216] For a description of the major toll roads currently in operation in England, see LOUISE BUTCHER, ROADS: TOLLS, HOUSE OF COMMONS LIBRARY STANDARD NOTE, Oct. 2013, SN442, http://www.parliament.uk/briefing-papers/ SN00442.pdf.

[217] Planning Act, 2008, c. 29, § 144, http://www.legislation.gov.uk/ukpga/2008/29/contents.

[218] BUTCHER, *supra* note 42, at 14.

[219] Transport Act, 2000, c. 38, http://www.legislation.gov.uk/ukpga/2000/38/contents.

[220] BUTCHER, *supra* note 42, at 8.

[221] *Id.* at 10.

[222] Transport Act, 2000, c. 38, § 163, http://www.legislation.gov.uk/ukpga/2000/38/contents.

[223] Greater London Authority Act, 1999, c. 29, § 295, http://www.legislation.gov.uk/ukpga/ 1999/29/contents.

[224] New Roads and Street Works Act, 1991, c. 22, http://www.legislation.gov.uk/ukpga/ 1991/22/contents.

[225] *Id.* § 1.

[226] *Road Tax to Be Scrapped*, SUNDAY EXPRESS (Sept. 23, 2012), http://www.express.co.uk/ news/uk/347695/Road- tax-to-be-scrapped.

[227] The Road User Charging (Charges and Penalty Charges) (London) Regulations, 2001, S.I. 2001/2285, http://www. legislation.gov.uk/uksi/2001/2285/pdfs/uksi_20012285_en.pdf.

[228] Greater London Authority Act, 1999, c. 29, § 295, http://www.legislation.gov.uk/ukpga/ 1999/29.

[229] *When to Pay,* TRANSPORT FOR LONDON, http://www.tfl.gov.uk/roadusers/ congestioncharging/ 17097.aspx (last visited Jan. 27, 2014).

[230] *Id.*

[231] Transport Act, 2000, c. 38, pt. III, http://www.legislation.gov.uk/ukpga/2000/38/contents.

[232] LOUISE BUTCHER, TRANSPORT INNOVATION FUND (TIF), 2005–2010, HOUSE OF COMMONS STANDARD NOTE, Aug. 2010, SN/BT/3711, http://www.parliament.uk/briefing-papers/SN03711.pdf.

[233] CODE DE LA VOIRIE ROUTIERE [CODE OF THE ROAD SYSTEM] arts. L111-1 & L121-1.

[234] *Id.* art. L121-1.

[235] The *départements,* which are governed by an elected general council, are the main territorial and administrative subdivisions of France (*Département*, ENCYCLOPÆDIA BRITANNICA ONLINE ACADEMIC EDITION, http://www.britannica.com/EBchecked/topic/158208/departement (last visited Jan. 24, 2014).

[236] CODE DE LA VOIRIE ROUTIERE arts. L111-1 & L131-1.

[237] *Id.* arts. L111-1 & L141-1.

[238] REPERES: CHIFFRES CLES DU TRANSPORT – ÉDITION 2013 [REFERENCES: KEY NUMBERS OF TRANSPORTATION –2013 EDITION], MINISTERE DE L'ECOLOGIE, DU DEVELOPPEMENT DURABLE, ET DE L'ENERGIE (Mar. 1, 2013), http://www.developpement-durable.gouv.fr/IMG/pdf/Rep_-_Chiffres_cles_transports_2013.pdf.

[239] *Id.*

[240] CODE DE LA VOIRIE ROUTIERE art. L111-1.

[241] CODE DE LA VOIRIE ROUTIERE art. L121-1.

[242] *Id.*

[243] *Id.* art. L123-1.

[244] *Les services routiers de l'Etat* [*The State's Road-Related Services*], MINISTERE DE L'ECOLOGIE, DU DEVELOPPEMENT DURABLE, ET DE L'ENERGIE (July 7, 2010), http://www.developpement-durable.gouv.fr/Presen tation-des-services-routiers.html.

[245] *Projets routiers* [*Road Projects*], MINISTERE DE L'ECOLOGIE, DU DEVELOPPEMENT DURABLE, ET DE L'ENERGIE (May 30, 2012), http://www.developpement-durable.gouv.fr/Le-financement-des-infrastructures.html.

[246] *Id.*

[247] *Id.*; Ordonnance no. 2004-559 du 17 juin 2004 sur les contrats de partenariat [Ordinance No. 2004-559 of June 17, 2004 on Partnership Contracts], JOURNAL OFFICIEL DE LA REPUBLIQUE FRANÇAISE [J.O.] [OFFICIAL GAZETTE OF FRANCE], June 19, 2004, p. 10994, art. 1.

[248] Décret no. 2004-1317 du 26 novembre 2004 relatif à l'Agence de financement des infrastructures de transport de France [Decree No. 2004-1317 of November 26, 2004, Regarding the Agency for the Funding of Transportation Infrastructure of France), J.O., Dec. 1, 2004, p.20474, art. 1; *Projets routiers*, *supra* note 24.

[249] Décret no. 2004-1317 du 26 novembre 2004 [Decree No. 2004-1317 of November 26, 2004] art. 5, *as modified by* Décret no. 2006-894 du 18 juillet 2006 modifiant le décret no. 2004-1317 du 26 novembre 2004 relatif à l'Agence de financement des infrastructures de transport de France [Decree No. 2006-894 of July 18, 2006, Regarding the Agency for the Funding of Transportation Infrastructure of France], J.O., July 20, 2006, p.10911, art. 3; *Projets routiers*, *supra* note 24.

[250] *Projets routiers*, *supra* note 13.

[251] CODE DE LA VOIRIE ROUTIERE art. L122-4.

[252] *Id.*

[253] *Id.*

[254] CODE DE LA VOIRIE ROUTIERE art. R*122-7.

[255] *Modalités de financement* [*Modes of Financing*], CAISSE NATIONALE DES AUTOROUTES, http://www.cna- autoroutes.fr/Modalite-de-financement.html?lang=fr (last visited Jan. 24, 2014).

[256] *Consistance et cartes du réseau routier national* [*Consistency and Maps of the National Road Network*], MINISTERE DE L'ECOLOGIE, DU DEVELOPPEMENT DURABLE, ET DE L'ENERGIE (June 10, 2013), http://www. developpement-durable.gouv.fr/Consistance-et-cartes-du-reseau.html.

[257] PRINCIPAUX TARIFS 2013 [PRINCIPAL RATES FOR 2013], ASSOCIATION DES SOCIETES FRANÇAISES D'AUTOROUTES [ASSOCIATION OF FRENCH HIGHWAY COMPANIES] (Feb. 2013), http://www.autoroutes.fr/FCKeditor/UserFiles/File/Tarifs%2022%20f%C3%A9vrier%202013.pdf.

[258] *Id.*

[259] Stephanie Fontaine, *Autoroutes: coup de chaud sur les prix des péages en France* [*Highways: Heat Wave on Toll Prices in France*], L'EXPRESS, July 23, 2013, http://votreargent.lexpress.fr/consommation/autoroutes-coup-de-chaud-sur-les-prix-des-peages-en-france_316039.html.

[260] *Principaux tarifs 2013*, *supra* note 25.

[261] *Les services routiers de l'Etat*, *supra* note 12.

[262] *Id.*

[263] Décret no. 2006-304 du 16 mars 2006 portant création et organisation des directions interdépartementales des routes [Decree No. 2006-304 of March 16, 2006, Creating and Organizing the Interdepartmental Directorates for Roads], J.O., Mar. 17, 2006, p.4048, art. 1; *Présentation de la DIR Atlantique* [*Introduction to DIR Atlantique*], DIR ATLANTIQUE, http://www.dir.atlantique.developpement-durable.gouv.fr/presentation-de-la-dir-atlantique-r1.html (last updated Jan. 24, 2014).

[264] Décret no. 2006-304 du 16 mars 2006 art. 3.

[265] CHRISTIAN ECKERT & ALAIN RODET, RAPPORT FAIT AU NOM DE LA COMMISSION DES FINANCES, DE L'ECONOMIE GENERALE ET DU CONTROLE BUDGETAIRE SUR LE PROJET DE LOI DE FINANCES POUR 2013, ANNEXE NO. 17 [REPORT FOR THE COMMISSION ON FINANCE, GENERAL ECONOMY, AND BUDGETARY CONTROL, ON THE PROPOSED BUDGETARY LAW FOR 2013, ANNEX NO. 17] 17, (Oct. 10, 2012), http://www.assemblee-nationale.fr/14/pdf/budget/ plf2013/b0251-tIII-a17.pdf.

[266] *Projets routiers*, *supra* note 13.

[267] *Répartition par type de route* [*Distribution According to Road Type*], MINISTERE DE L'ECOLOGIE, DU DEVELOPPEMENT DURABLE, ET DE L'ENERGIE, http://www.developpement-durable.gouv.fr/ Repartition-par-type-de- route (last updated Oct. 21, 2013).

[268] CODE DE LA VOIRIE ROUTIERE art. L122-4.

[269] *Répartition par type de route*, *supra* note 35.

[270] *Id.*

[271] CODE DE LA VOIRIE ROUTIERE art. L131-2.

[272] CODE GENERAL DES COLLECTIVITES TERRITORIALES [GENERAL CODE OF REGIONAL AND LOCAL AUTHORITIES] art. L3321-1(16).

[273] *Id.* arts. L3336-1 & L2337-3.

[274] *Id.* arts. L3212-1–L3212-2.

[275] *Id.* art. L3332-1(5).

[276] *Id.* art. L2321-2(20); CODE DE LA VOIRIE ROUTIERE art. L141-8.

[277] CODE GENERAL DES COLLECTIVITES TERRITORIALES arts. L2331-1–L2331-10.

[278] *Id.* arts. L5111-1 & L5210-1-1A.

[279] *Id.* art. L5111-1.

[280] *Id.* arts. L3212-3 & L3332-3(6).

[281] *Id.* arts. L3332-3(6), L3334-10–L3334-12.

[282] *Taxe poids lourds (TPL ou écotaxe)* [*Heavy Truck Tax (TPL or Ecotax)*], SERVICE-PUBLIC.FR, http://vosdroits. service-public.fr/professionnels-entreprises/F31213.xhtml (last updated Dec. 12, 2013).

[283] *Id.*

[284] *Id.*

[285] Stanislas du Guerny, *La Bretagne reste vent debout contre l'écotaxe pour les poids lourds* [*Brittany Remains Up in Arms Against the Ecotaxe on Heavy Trucks*], LES ECHOS (Oct. 27, 2013), http://www.lesechos.fr/economie-politique/politique/actu/0203092773914-la-bretagne-reste-vent-debout-contre-l-ecotaxe-pour-les-poids-lourds-622721.php.

[286] Jean-Marc Ayrault, Premier ministre [Prime Minister], Déclaration de à l'issue de la réunion avec les élus Bretons [Declaration After Meeting with Breton Elected Officials] (Oct. 29, 2013), http://www.gouvernement.fr/sites/default/files/interventions/10.29_discours_de_jean-marc_ayrault_premier_ministre_a_lissue_de_la_reunion_ avec_les_elus_bretons.pdf.

[287] Cyrille Pluyette, *L'écotaxe devrait être décalée d'un an* [*The Ecotaxe Will Probably Be Pushed Back One Year*], LE FIGARO (Nov. 29, 2013), http://www.lefigaro.fr /conjoncture/2013/11/ 29/20002-20131129ARTFIG00572-l- ecotaxe-devrait-etre-decalee-d-un-an.php.

[288] GRUNDGESETZ FÜR DIE BUNDESREPUBLIK DEUTSCHLAND [BASIC LAW] art. 90, *translation at* http://www.gesetze-im-internet.de/englisch_gg/englisch_gg.html; Bundesfernstrassengesetz [Federal Long-Distance Highway Act], *repromulgated* June 28, 2007, BUNDESGESETZBLATT [BGBL.] I at 1206, *as amended*, § 1, http://www.gesetze-im-internet.de/fstrg/BJNR009030953.html.

[289] Robert Uerpmann-Wittzach, *Verkehr*, in 4 HANDBUCH DES STAATSRECHTS 796 (Josef Isensee & Paul Kirchhof eds., 2006).

[290] BASIC LAW art. 90.

[291] BASIC LAW art. 85; Bundeshaushaltsplan 2013 [2013 Federal Budget], Strassenbauplan 2013 [Road Construction Plan 2013], 1210, p. 27, http://www.bundeshaushalt-info.de/fileadmin/de.bundeshaushalt/content_de/dokumente/2013/soll/Haushaltsplan-2013.pdf.

[292] BASIC LAW art. 104a.

[293] BASIC LAW art. 106.

[294] Strassenbaufinanzierungsgesetz [Highway Construction Financing Act], Mar. 28, 1960, BGBL. I at 201, *as last amended* by Verordnung, Oct. 31, 2006, BGBL. I at 2407, art. 3.

[295] Gesetz über die Erhebung von streckenbezogenen Gebühren für die Benutzung von Bundesautobahnen und Bundesstrassen [Federal Highway Toll Act], July 12, 2011, BGBL. I at 1378, § 11.

[296] Energiesteuergesetz [Energy Tax Act], July 15, 2006, BGBL. I at 1534, *as amended*, § 2.

[297] Kraftfahrzeugsteuergesetz [Motor Vehicle Tax Act], *repromulgated* Sept. 26, 2002, BGBL. I at 3818, *as amended*, http://www.gesetze-im-internet.de/kraftstg/BJNR005090927.html.

[298] BASIC LAW art. 106(1), Nos. 2 and 3.

[299] Walter Schulz, *Handwerk kämpft für Meistertitel; ABRECHNUNG Beim Jahresempfang der Kreishandwerkschaft fielen deutliche Worte,* KÖLNER STADT-ANZEIGER 44 (Jan. 11, 2014), *available at* Lexis (by subscription).

[300] Mineralölsteuergesetz [Mineral Oil Tax Act], *repromulgated* Dec. 20, 1988, BGBL. I at 2277, *as amended.*

[301] Highway Construction Financing Act art. 1.

[302] Energy Tax Act art. 3.

[303] Michail Hengstenberg, *Streitthema Autobahngebühr: Seehofer erneuert Forderung nach Maut für Ausländer,* SPIEGEL ONLINE (Sept. 8, 2013), http://www.spiegel.de/politik/deutschland/pkw-maut-seehofer-erneuert-forderung- nach-der-maut-fuer-auslaender-a-921050.html.

[304] *Id.*

[305] *Verkehrsministerkonfeenz – Milliarden für Sanierung marode Strassen*, MITTELDEUTSCHER RUNDFUNK, http://www.mdr.de/nachrichten/verkehrsministerkonferenz102.html (last visited Jan. 22, 2014).

[306] *The Open Budget: Development of Transportation*, ISRAEL GOVERNMENT PORTAL, http://budget.msh.gov.il/#0079, 2014,0,1,1,1,0,0,0,0,0,0 (scroll down to 2013 and to 2014; in Hebrew; last visited Jan. 6, 2014).

[307] Information on the MTNIRS is posted on the Ministry's website, at http://en.mot.gov.il/about-mot-cbl/5-minister- katz (last visited Jan. 7, 2014).

[308] MTNIRS, BUDGET PRINCIPLES FOR 2013–2014, at 165, http://www.mof.gov.il/BudgetSite/StateBudget/Budget2013_2014/MinisteriesBudget/Foundations/Lists/List3/Attachments/1/Tahabora_Main.pdf (in Hebrew).

[309] *Netivei Israel – National Transport Infrastructure Company Ltd.*, BDICOFACE, http://www.bdicode.co.il/CompanyTextProfile_ENG/1940_694_0/Netivei%20Israel%20%e2%80%93%20National%20Transport%20Infrastr ucture%20Company%20Ltd (last visited Jan. 6, 2014).

[310] *See Who Are We*, NETIVEI ISRAEL, http://iroads.co.il/he/about (translated from Hebrew by author, R.L.; last visited Jan. 6, 2014).

[311] *Id.*

[312] *Id.*

[313] *Implementing Authority and the Concessionaire*, KVISH HOZE ISRAEL, http://www.hozeisrael.co.il/template/default.asp?PageId=66&catId=12&maincat=6 (in Hebrew; last visited Jan 6, 2014).

[314] Yehuda Ravehet et. al., *Cross-Israel Highway Leads the Way to Public-Private Partnerships*, INTERNATIONAL LAW OFFICE (ILO) (Nov. 19, 2002), http://www.internationallawoffice.com/newsletters/detail.aspx?g=da09f7a9-f8e1-4c88-8dfd-251ef254b4bb&redir=1. The article provides additional information on financing and operations.

[315] KVISH HOZE ISRAEL, *supra* note 8.

[316] *Id.*

[317] MINISTRY OF FINANCE, BUDGET PRINCIPLES FOR 2011–2012, at 252, http://www.mof.gov.il/BudgetSite/StateBudget/Budget2011_2012/Lists/List4/Attachments/1/ekronotHok_2011_12.pdf; *see also* YNET LEXICON FOR ECONOMICS, http://www.yediothsfarim.co.il/lexicons/econ/glossary/g_691.asp (both in Hebrew; last visited Dec. 24, 2013).

[318] *See* BUDGET PRINCIPLES FOR 2013–2014, *supra* note 3.

[319] Toll Road (Israel National Highway) Law 5755-1995, SEFER HAHUKIM [SH] [OFFICIAL GAZETTE] 5755 No. 1545 p. 490, as amended (in Hebrew).

[320] *Id.* § 2.

[321] *Id.* §§ 3–5, 11.

[322] *Id.* §§ 6, 7.

[323] *Id.* §§ 12–12D.

[324] BUDGET PRINCIPLES FOR 2013–2014, *supra* note 3.

[325] *See* Part II(B)(2) of this report.

[326] Toll Road (Israel National Highway) Law 5755-1995, SH 5755 No. 1545 p. 490, *as amended* (in Hebrew).

[327] For specific figures, see AVICHAI ODESAR, MINISTRY OF FINANCE, TAXATION OF VEHICLES ch. 14, http://govx.mof.gov.il/Lists/List26/Attachments/491/%D7%A4%D7%A8%D7%A7%20%D7%9E%D7%99%D7%A1%D7%95%D7%99%20%D7%A8%D7%9B%D7%91.docx (in Hebrew; last visited Dec. 31, 2013).

[328] *Details Regarding Support for Implementation of Payments and Reporting*, PURCHASE AND EXCISE TAXES- ISRAEL TAX AUTHORITY, http://taxes.gov.il/OTHERINDIRECTTAXES/Pages/TaxesIndirectTaxLobby.aspx (translated from Hebrew by author, R.L; last visited Jan. 6, 2014),

[329] For general information on the Purchase Tax, see ISRAEL TAX AUTHORITY, http://taxes.gov.il/OtherIndirectTaxes/Pages/TaxesAAPurchaseTax.aspx (in Hebrew; last visited Jan. 7, 2014).

[330] Purchase Tax (Goods and Services) Law, 5712-1952, SH No. 110 p. 344.

[331] ODESAR, *supra* note 24, at 2 (translated by R.L.).

[332] *Id.*

[333] *Id.*

[334] For additional information on and links to the text of Israel's FTA agreements, see *Trade Agreements and Bilateral Issues*, MINISTRY OF INDUSTRY, TRADE AND LABOR, http://www.moit.gov.il/NR/exeres/00E158D1-2672-4B9F-B35C-29D4A6D56009.htm (last visited Jan. 7, 2014).

[335] ISRAEL TAX AUTHORITY, THE STATE OF ISRAEL, MINISTRY OF FINANCE, GUIDE FOR INDIVIDUAL IMPORT OF VEHICLES 4 (updated to Aug. 5, 2013, http://taxes.gov.il/customs/PersonalImport/Documents/MadrihYevu IshiRehev.pdf (in Hebrew).

[336] *Id.* at 4–5.

[337] Value Added Tax Law, 5736-1975, 30 LAWS OF THE STATE OF ISRAEL 46 (5736-1975/76), *as amended.*

[338] Decree on Value Added Tax (Rate of Tax on a Transaction and on Import of Goods), 5765-2005, *as amended*, § 1, KOVETZ HATAKANOT [KT] [SUBSIDIARY LEGISLATION] No. 6416 p. 913; *see also* Yoel Shwarz, *VAT [for] Cars More Expensive* , AUTO.CO.IL (June 2, 2013), http://www.auto.co.il/כתבה-30073-המע -מ-מייקר-את-המכוניות.aspx (both in Hebrew).

[339] *Rates of Indirect Tax on Gasoline*, ISRAEL TAX AUTHORITY (updated to Apr. 30, 2014), http://taxes.gov.il/OtherIndirectTaxes/Documents/DelekSoler/delek300414.docx (in Hebrew).

[340] Avi Bar-Eli, *Tax on Gasoline will increase in 6 Agorot for Liter*, THE MARKER (Aug. 21, 2013), http://www.the marker.com/dynamo/1.2103071 (in Hebrew).

[341] ODESAR, *supra* note 24, at 8.

[342] *Id.*

[343] CONSTITUTION OF THE ITALIAN REPUBLIC (English version published by the Parliamentary Information, Archives and Publications Office of the Senate Service for Official Reports and Communication of the Senato della Repubblica, Apr. 2009), http://www.senato.it/documenti/repository/istituzione/costituzione _inglese.pdf.

[344] *Id.* art. 117, paras. 1& 2.

[345] *Id.* art. 117, para. 3.

[346] Decreto Legge [D.L.] 25 settembre 2009, n. 135, Disposizioni urgenti per l'attuazione di obblighi comunitari e per l'esecuzione di sentenze della Corte di giustizia delle Comunita' europee [Decree Law No. 135 of September 25, 2009, Urgent Provisions for the Implementation of Community Obligations and for the Execution of the European Court of Justice's Decisions], GAZETTA UFFICIALE [G.U.] [OFFICIAL GAZETTE] No. 223, Oct. 25, 2009, http://www.normattiva.it/uri-res/N2Ls?urn:nir:stato:decreto.legge:2009;135~art19 quater.

[347] D.L. n. 135 of 2009 art. 3-ter.

[348] Decreto Legge 31 maggio 2010, n. 78, Misure urgenti in materia di stabilizzazione finanziaria e di competitivita' economica [Decree Law No. 78 of May 31, 2010, Urgent Measures Concerning Financial and Economic Competitiveness Stability], art. 8, paras. 1–5, G.U. No. 125, May 31, 2010, http://www.normattiva.it/uri-res/N2Ls?urn:nir:stato:decreto.legge:2010-05-31;78!vig=.

[349] This system became operational on April 30, 2011. *See* Decreto Legge 5 agosto 2010, n. 125, Misure urgenti per il settore dei trasporti e disposizioni in materia finanziaria [Decree Law No. 125 of August 5, 2010, Urgent Measures for the Transportation Sector and Concerning Financial Matters], G.U. No. 182, Aug. 6, 2010, http://www.norm attiva.it/uri-res/N2Ls?urn:nir:stato:decreto.legge:2010-08-05;125!vig.

[350] *Redazione ed Approvazione del Bilancio Dello Stato Italiano [Preparation and Approval of the Italian State Budget]*, LIBERO, http://digilander.libero.it/lancenia/Il_bilancio_dello _Stato _ italiano.htm (last visited Feb. 6, 2014).

[351] Legge 27 dicembre 2013, n. 147, Disposizioni per la formazione del bilancio annuale e pluriennale dello Stato (Legge di stabilita' 2014) [Law 147 of December 27, 2013, Provisions for the Preparation of the Annual and Pluriannual Budget of the State (Stability Law of 2014)], G.U. No. 302, Dec. 27, 2013, http://www.normattiva.it/uri- res/N2Ls?urn:nir:stato:legge:2013;147.

[352] *Id.* art. 1, No. 68.

[353] *Id.* art. 1, No. 81; *see also* Decreto Legge 6 luglio 2011, n. 98, Disposizioni urgenti per la stabilizzazione finanziaria [Decree Law 98 of July 6, 2011, Urgent Provisions for Financial Stability] art. 32, para. 1, G.U. No. 155, July 6, 2011, http://www.normattiva.it/uri-res/N2Ls?urn:nir:stato:decreto.legge:2011-07-06;98 (creating, under the Ministry of

Infrastructure and Transportation, the railroad and highway infrastructure related to the Strategic Interest Works Fund, appropriating €930 million [about US$1,271,000] for fiscal year (FY) 2012 and €1,000 million [about US$1,367,000] for FYs 2013 to 2016).

[354] Legge 21 dicembre 2001, n. 443, Delega al Governo in materia di infrastrutture ed insediamenti produttivi strategici ed altri interventi per il rilancio delle attivita' produttive [Law 443 of December 21, 2001, Delegating in the Government the Concerning Infrastructure and Strategic Production and Other Investments for the Revival of Productive Activity], G.U. No. 299, Dec. 27, 2001, http://www.normattiva.it/uri-res/N2Ls?urn:nir: stato: legge:2001;443.

[355] *Temi dell'attività Parlamentare: Le infrastrutture strategiche* [*Topics of Parliamentary Activity: Strategic Infrastructure*], PARLAMENTO ITALIANO, http://leg16.camera.it/465? area=32&tema=71&Le+infrastrutture+ strategiche (last visited Feb. 6, 2014).

[356] The documents composing the *Infrastructure Annex* are called "documents of economics and finance," pursuant to Legge 7 aprile 2011, n. 39 Modifiche alla legge 31 dicembre 2009, n. 196, conseguenti alle nuove regole adottate dall'Unione europea in materia di coordinamento delle politiche economiche degli Stati membri [Law 39 of April 7, 2011, Amending Law 196 of December 31, 2009, Arising from the New Rules Adopted by the European Union Concerning the Coordination of the Economic Policies of the Member States], G.U. No. 84, Apr. 12, 2011, http://www.normattiva.it/uri-res/N2Ls?urn:nir: stato:legge:2011;39.

[357] *Id.* In addition to fuels, the excise is applied to gas, electricity, alcohol, and tobacco.

[358] Vehicles with a low environmental impact—such as hybrid electric vehicles fueled exclusively by GLP (natural gas) or methane sources— may take advantage of a large tax reduction. Also, vehicles of historical interest that are enrolled in special registries are subject to the payment of a reduced rate ("Minitax"), payable only in the case of effective use, and disabled persons have a right to a complete exemption from the tax if their vehicle is adapted to the particular type of disability. In addition, the so-called "Supertax," applicable since 2012, is an additional increment of the automobile tax on passenger cars and motor vehicles used for the transportation of persons and goods, which applies to two large categories: (a) vehicles with power above 225 Kw acquired between July 7 and December 31, 2011; and (b) vehicles with more than 185 Kw registered after 2008, which had to comply with the new rules before January 31, 2012. Legge 14 giugno 1990, n. 158, Norme di delega in materia di autonomia impositiva delle regioni e altre disposizioni concernenti i rapporti finanziari tra lo Stato e le regioni [Law 158 of June 14, 1990, Norm for the Delegation of Powers Concerning the Tax Autonomy of the Regions and Other Provisions Related to the Financial Relationship Between the State and the Regions] art. 4, G.U. No. 144, June 22, 1990, http://www.normattiva.it/uri-res/N2Ls?urn:nir:stato: legge:1990-06-14;158. Finally, effective in 2011, passenger cars and motor vehicles used for the transportation of persons and goods with power higher than 225 Kw are subject to an additional increment over the tax introduced by D.L. 98, *supra* note 11, which was converted into law by Legge 15 luglio 2011, n. 111. [Law No. 111 of July 15, 2011] art. 23, para. 21, G.U. No. 164 of July 16, 2011, http://www.normattiva.it/uri-res/N2Ls?urn: nir:stato: legge:2011-07-15;111!vig=.].

[359] Legge 24 dicembre 1993, n. 537, Interventi correttivi di finanza pubblica [Law No. 537 of December 24, 1993, Corrective Actions of Public Finance] art. 10, para. 3, G.U. No. 393, Dec. 28, 1993, http://www.normattiva.it/uri- res/N2Ls?urn:nir:stato:legge:1993-12-24;537.

[360] Legge 27 dicembre 2006, n. 296, Disposizioni per la formazione del bilancio annuale e pluriennale dello Stato (legge finanziaria 2007) [Law 296 of December 27, 2006, Provisions for the Formation of the Annual and Pluriannual Budget of the State (Financial Law of 2007)] art. 1, para. 1020, G.U. No. 299, Dec. 27, 2006, http://www.normattiva.it/uri-res/N2Ls?urn:nir:stato:legge:2006-12-27;296!vig=; Decreto Legge 23 ottobre 2008, n. 162, Interventi urgenti in materia di adeguamento dei prezzi di materiali da costruzione, di sostegno ai settori dell'autotrasporto, dell'agricoltura e della pesca professionale, nonche' di

finanziamento delle opere per il G8 e definizione degli adempimenti tributari per le regioni Marche ed Umbria, colpite dagli eventi sismici del 1997 [Decree Law No. 162 of October 23, 2008, Urgent Action Concerning the Adjustment of Prices of Building Materials, Support of the Road Sectors, Agriculture and Professional Fishing, as well as Financing of the Works for the G8, and Definition of Tax Compliance for the Regions of Umbria and Marche, Affected by the Earthquake of 1997] art. 19, para. 9-bis, G.U. No. 249, Oct. 23, 2008, http://www.normattiva.it/uri-res/N2Ls?urn:nir:stato:decreto-%20%20%20%20%20%20%20%20%20%20%20%20legge:2008;162; D.L. 78 of 2009, *supra* note 6, art. 5(7).

[361] *See* Decreto Legge 8 aprile 2008, n. 59 Disposizioni urgenti per l'attuazione di obblighi comunitari e l'esecuzione di sentenze della Corte di giustizia delle Comunita' europee [Decree Law No. 59 of April 8, 2008, Urgent Provisions for the Implementation of Community Obligations and for the Execution of the European Court of Justice's Decisions] art. 8-duodecies, G.U. No. 84, Apr. 9, 2008, http://www.normattiva.it/uri-res/N2Ls?urn:nir:stato: decreto.legge:2008;59 (introducing a new tariff adjustment mechanism between tolls to both the effective inflation rate of the preceding year and the return on investments).

[362] For more information on Highway Concessions by ANAS, see Camera dei deputati, XVI Legislatura, Documentazione e ricerche, L'Anas e le concessioni autostradali [ANAS and Highway Concessions], n. 249, July 6, 2011, http://documenti.camera.it/leg16/dossier/Testi/Am0234.htm#dossierList.

[363] Decreto Legge 6 dicembre 2011, n. 201, Disposizioni urgenti per la crescita, l'equita' e il consolidamento dei conti pubblici [Decree Law No. 201 of December 6, 2011, Urgent Provisions for the Growth, Equity, and Consolidation of Public Accounts] art. 42, paras. 6 & 7, G.U. No. 284, Dec. 6, 2011, http://www.normattiva.it/uri-res/N2Ls?urn:nir:stato: decreto.legge:2011;201.

[364] Decreto Legge 24 gennaio 2012, n. 1, Disposizioni urgenti per la concorrenza, lo sviluppo delle infrastrutture e la competitivita' [Decree Law No. 1 of January 24, 2012, Urgent Provisions for Competition, Development of Infrastructure and Competitiveness] art. 41, G.U. No. 19, Jan. 24, 2012, http://www.normattiva.it/atto/caricaDettaglioAtto?atto.dataPubblicazione Gazzetta=2012-01-24&atto.codiceRedazionale=012G0009, *amended by* Decreto Legge 22 giugno 2012, n. 83, Misure urgenti per la crescita del Paese [Decree Law No. 83 of June 22, 2012, Urgent Measures for the Growth of the Country] art. 1, G.U. No. 187, Aug. 11, 2012, http://www.normattiva. it/uri- res/N2Ls?urn:nir:stato: decreto.legge:2012-06-22;83.

[365] D.L. 201 of 2011, *supra* note 22, art. 41, para. 5-bis (regulating the adjudicating authority, the submission of proposals, and the procedure for the financing of infrastructure projects).

[366] Legge 12 novembre 2011, n. 183, Disposizioni per la formazione del bilancio annuale e pluriennale dello Stato(Legge di stabilita' 2012) [Law 183 of November 12, 2011, Provisions for the Formation of the Annual and Pluriannual Budget of the State (Stability Law of 2012)] art. 18, G.U. No. 265, Nov. 14, 2011, http://www.norm attiva.it/uri-res/N2Ls?urn:nir:stato:legge:2011-11-12;183.

[367] Decreto Legge 18 ottobre 2012, n. 179 Ulteriori misure urgenti per la crescita del Paese [Decree Law No. 179 of October 18, 2012, Further Urgent Measures for the Country's Growth] art. 33 et seq., G.U. No. 245, Oct. 19, 2012, http://www.normattiva.it/uri-res/N2Ls?urn:nir:stato:decreto-legge:2012-10-18;179!vig.

[368] Dōro hō [Road Law], Act No. 180 of 1952, *amended by* Act No. 30 of 2013, art. 12.

[369] Kokudo keisei keikaku hō [National Spatial Planning Act], Act No. 205 of 1950, *amended by* Act No. 89 of 2005, art. 2, para. 1, item 6; Kokudo kaihatsu kansen jidōshadō kensetsu hō [Act on Construction of Arterial Roads for Land Development], Act No. 68 of 1957, *last amended by* Act No. 160 of 1999, art. 3 & attached table.

[370] The 5th Comprehensive National Development Plan, Grand Design for the 21st Century, Cabinet Decision (Mar. 31, 1998), http://www.mlit.go.jp/kokudokeikaku/zs5-e/.

[371] Road Law arts. 3, 3-2 & 48-2. *See also* MLIT, Expressways in Japan, Presentation, at 4, http://www.mlit.go.jp/road/road_e/03key_challenges/6-1.pdf (last visited Jan. 27, 2014).
[372] Act on Construction of Arterial Roads for Land Development art. 3 & attached table.
[373] *Id.* art. 5, para. 1.
[374] *Id.* art. 11.
[375] *Id.* art. 13.
[376] Kōsoku jidōsha kokudō hō [National Highway Act], Act No. 79 of 1957, *amended by* Act No. 76 of 2013, art. 5.
[377] Dōro seibi tokubetsu sochi hō [Special Act on Road Construction and Maintenance], Act No. 7 of 1956, *last amended by* Act No. 101 of 2004, art. 3.
[378] Special Act on Road Construction and Maintenance, Act No. 7 of 1956, art. 2-2, *as amended by* Act No. 80 of 1957.
[379] Nihon dōro kōdan hō [Japan Highway Public Corporation Act], Act No. 6 of 1956.
[380] *Welcome to JH*, Japan Highway Public Corporation (JH), http://warp.da.ndl.go.jp/info:ndljp/pid/236639/www.jhnet.go.jp/english_new/ (Jan. 1, 2005). The website was archived by the National Diet Library of Japan.
[381] Dōro seibi tokubetsu sochi hō [Special Act on Road Construction and Maintenance], Act No. 169 of 1952, art. 3. This Act was abolished by the Act of the same name referenced in note 10.
[382] Takaaki Nambu, Roads Fund Board, United Republic of Tanzania, *Histry [sic] of Road Development, Finance and Investment in Japan*, at 8, http://www.roadsfundtz.org/web/pdf/session%204/Japan%20History%20of%20Road%20Development%20Finance%20and%20%20%20%20%20%20Investment.pdf (last visited Jan. 3, 2014).
[383] *Id.*
[384] Chihō dōro kōsha hō [Local Road Public Corporation Act], Act No. 82 of 1970.
[385] Fumitoshi Mizutani & Shuji Uranishi, Privatization of the Japan Highway Public Corporation: Policy Assessment, Paper for the 46th Congress for the European Regional Science Association, at 11 (2006), http://www-sre.wu- wien.ac.at/ersa/ersaconfs/ersa06/papers/226.pdf.
[385] *Id.* at 14.
[386] *Id.* at 11.
[387] *Promotion Committee for the Privatization of the Four Highway-related Public Corporations*, PRIME MINISTER OF JAPAN AND HIS CABINET, http://www.kantei.go.jp/foreign/policy/road/index_e.html (last visited Jan. 21, 2014).
[388] Promotion Committee for the Privatization of the Four Highway-related Public Corporations, Comments (summary) (Dec. 6, 2002), http://www.kantei.go.jp/foreign/policy/2002/021206iken_s_e.pdf (copy and paste URL into browser).
[389] Nobuhiro Yamagoshi, *Doro kankei yon kodan mineika no kensho* [*Examination of Privatization of Four Public Corporations Relating to Roads*], RIPPŌ TO CHŌSA No. 260, at 35, 37–38 (Oct. 2006), http://www.sangiin.go.jp/japanese/annai/chousa/rippou_chousa/backnumber/2006pdf/20061006035.pdf.
[390] *President's Message*, JEHDRA (Sept. 2013), http://www.jehdra.go.jp/english/president.html.
[391] Dokuritsu gyōsei hōjin nihon kōsoku dōro hoyū·saimu hensai kikō hō [Japan Expressways Holding and Debt Repayment Agency Act], Act No. 100 of 2004, *last amended by* Act No. 66 of 2006, art. 12.
[392] JOSÉ MANUEL VASSALLO, EXECUTIVE REPORT: ANALYSIS OF THE JAPANESE TOLL EXPRESSWAY SYSTEM IN THE FRAMEWORK OF THE CURRENT TREND OF THE TOLL ROAD BUSINESS IN THE WORLD 133 (Nov. 2008), http://www.jehdra.go.jp/english/pdf/others/107.pdf.
[393] *Id.*
[394] *Gyōmu no gaiyō* [*Summary of Our Business*], JEHDRA, http://www.jehdra.go.jp/gyoumunogaiyou.html (last visited Jan. 7, 2014).
[395] Promotion Committee, *supra* note 22, at 2-3.

[396] MLIT, KŌSOKU JIDŌSHA KOKUDŌ NO HYŌKA KEKKA NI TSUITE [REGARDING EVALUATION RESULTS OF NATIONAL EXPRESSWAYS] 1, http://www.mlit.go.jp/kisha/kisha03/06/061128_2/02.pdf (last visited Jan. 17, 2014). National Highway Act and Okinawa Promotion Special Measures Act Amendment, Act No. 36 of 2003.

[397] MLIT, MAINTENANCE STANDARDS OF GENERAL NATIONAL ROADS AND NATIONAL EXPRESSWAYS THAT THE NATIONAL GOVERNMENT MANAGES (DRAFT) 1, http://www.mlit.go.jp/road/ir/ir-council/pdf/iji1_1.pdf (in Japanese).

[398] MLIT Presentation, *supra* note 4, at 4.

[399] Road Law, Act No. 180 of 1952, *amended by* Act No. 30 of 2013, art. 12.

[400] JEHDRA Act, Act No. 100 of 2004, art. 22, para. 1.

[401] *Id.* art. 23.

[402] The funds for FILP bonds are "procured through the government bond issuance supply resources to Fiscal Loans of the Fiscal Loan Fund and their principal and interest repayment is covered by returns from these loans, while ordinary government bonds supply resources to expenditures of the General Account and their repayment is covered by taxation etc." *How Do FILP Bonds Differ from Government Bonds?*, MINISTRY OF FINANCE, http://www.mof.go.jp/english/filp/filp_report/zaito2010/zaito2010-4-04.html (last visited Jan. 13, 2014).

[403] JEHDRA Act, Act No. 100 of 2004, *last amended by* Act No. 66 of 2006, art. 12, paras. 4–6 & art. 25.

[405] National Highway Act art. 20, para. 1.

[406] Road Law, Act No. 180 of 1952, *amended by* Act No. 30 of 2013, art. 50, para. 1.

[407] Road Law art. 49.

[408] Mizutani & Uranishi, *supra* note 18, at 2.

[409] JEHDRA Act, Act No. 100 of 2004, art. 16.

[410] *Id.* art. 13; *see also* VASSALLO, *supra* note 26, at 133.

[411] Kazuaki Nagata, *A Highway System that Ever Exacts Toll*, JAPAN TIMES (Dec. 16, 2008), http://www.japantimes.co.jp/news/2008/12/16/news/a-highway-system-that-ever-exacts-toll/. *See also* MLIT, Changes of Highway Pricing System in Other Countries, Hand-out at the 9th Meeting of Experts Committee on Highway System 3 (Aug. 22, 2011), http://www.mlit.go.jp/road/ir/ir-council/hw_arikata/pdf9/6.pdf (in Japanese).

[412] *Tsūkō ryōkin sisutemu* [*Toll System*], CENTRAL NIPPON EXPRESSWAY COMPANY LIMITED, http://www.c- nexco.co.jp/shintomei/images/toll/02.pdf (in Japanese; last visited Jan 21, 2014).

[413] Nambu, *supra* note 15, at 6.

[414] Temporary Special Measures Act on Financial Source of Road Construction, Act No. 73 of 1953.

[415] *Id.* art. 3.

[416] Local Gasoline Tax Act, Act No. 104 of 1955, *amended by* Act No. 114 of 2011.

[417] Local Tax Act Amendment, Act No. 81 of 1956, art. 700.

[418] Liquefied Petroleum Gas Tax Act, Act No. 156 of 1965.

[419] Local Tax Act Amendment, Act No. 4 of 1968.

[420] Motor Vehicle Tonnage Tax Act, Act No. 89 of 1971.

[421] Dōro seibi tokubetsu kaikei hō [Act on Special Account for Road Construction], Act No. 35 of 1958.

[422] Gasoline Tax Act, Act No. 55 of 1957, art. 3.

[423] *Id.* art. 9; Tax Special Measures Act, Act No. 26 of 1957, *amended by* Act No. 45 of 2013 art. 88-8.

[424] Local Gasoline Tax Act, Act No. 104 of 1955, *amended by* Act No. 114 of 2011, art. 4; Tax Special Measures Act art. 88-8.

[425] Local Tax Act, Act No. 226 of 1950, *amended by* Act No. 63 of 2013, art. 144-2; *see also* *Keiyu Torihiki Zei* [*Diesel Fuel Transaction Tax*], BUREAU OF TAXATION, TOKYO

METROPOLITAN GOVERNMENT, http://www.tax.metro.tokyo.jp/shitsumon/tozei/index_n.htm (last visited Jan. 14, 2014).

[426] Local Tax Act art. 144-10.

[427] Liquefied Petroleum Gas Tax Act art. 4.

[428] *Id.* art. 10.

[429] Nambu, *supra* note 15, at 5.

[430] Local Tax Act art. 118.

[431] *Id.* art. 119; Supplemental Provisions art. 12-2-3.

[432] LIBERAL DEMOCRATIC PARTY & KOMEI PARTY, SUMMARY OF TAX REFORM IN FISCAL YEAR 2014 at 97 (Dec. 12, 2013), http://jimin.ncss.nifty.com/pdf/zeisei2013/pdf128_1.pdf (in Japanese).

[433] *Id.* at 4.

[434] Motor Vehicle Tonnage Tax Act, Act No. 89 of 1971, *amended by* Act No. 53 of 2013, art. 4.

[435] *Corolla Fielder Specification*, TOYOTA, http://toyota.jp/corollafielder/003_p_003/ spec/ spec/ gasoline/2wd/ (last visited Jan. 16, 2014).

[436] *Specification LS460/LS460L*, LEXUS, http://lexus.jp/models/ls/specifications/specifications/ ls460/index.html (last visited Jan. 16, 2014).

[437] Motor Vehicle Tonnage Act art. 7; Tax Special Measures Act, Act No. 26 of 1957, *amended by* Act No. 45 of 2013 arts. 90-11, 90-11-2 & 90-12. *See also Jidosha juryo zei* [*Motor Vehicle Tonnage Tax*], *Shaken to kuruma no tetuduki annai senta* [*Car Inspection and Other Car Procedures Guidance Center*], DISTRICT TRANSPORT SUB- BUREAU, http://annai-center.com/ documents/juryozei.php (last visited Jan. 16, 2014).

[438] *Doro tokutei zaigen no ippan zaigenka ni tsuite* [*Regarding Making Road-Specific Revenue Source Into General Revenue Source*], MLIT, http://www.mlit.go.jp/road/ir/ir-funds/minaoshi.html (last visited Jan. 16, 2014).

[439] Ley de Caminos, Puentes y Autotransporte Federal [Law of Roads, Bridges and Federal Motor Transportation], art. 2, DIARIO OFICIAL [D.O.], Dec. 22, 1993, *as amended*, http://www.diputados.gob.mx/LeyesBiblio/pdf/27.pdf.

[440] *Id.* art. 5.

[441] CONSTITUCIÓN POLÍTICA DE LOS ESTADOS UNIDOS MEXICANOS [POLITCAL CONSTITUTION OF THE UNITED MEXICAN STATES], *as amended*, art. 117(IV), D.O., Feb. 5, 1917, http://www.diputados.gob.mx/LeyesBiblio/ pdf/1.pdf (translated by the author).

[442] César Alberto Cortés Prado, Metodología Para la Selección de Alternativas de Conservación de Carreteras, Usando el Modelo HDM-4 (2005) (unpublished civil engineering degree thesis, Universidad de las Américas, Puebla), *available at* http://catarina.udlap.mx/u_dl_a/ tales/documentos/lic/cortes_p_ca/.

[443] Presupuesto de Egresos de la Federación para el Ejercicio Fiscal 2014 [Federal Budget Expenditures for Fiscal 2014], D.O., Dec. 3, 2013, http://www.diputados.gob.mx/ LeyesBiblio/pdf/PEF_2014.pdf.

[444] Cortés Prado, *supra* note 4.

[445] Michael D. Plante & Amy Jordan, *Getting Prices Right: Addressing Mexico's History of Fuel Subsidies*, *in* FEDERAL RESERVE BANK OF DALLAS, SOUTHWEST ECONOMY: THIRD QUARTER 2013 at 10, 11 & 13, *available at* http://www.dallasfed.org/assets/documents/ research/swe/2013/ swe1303d.pdf.

[446] Decreto por el que se Expide la Ley de Ingresos para el Ejercicio Fiscal de 2014, y se Reforma el Primer Párrafo del Artículo 2 de la Ley de Ingresos de la Federación para el Ejercicio Fiscal de 2013 [Decree on the Revenue Act for Fiscal Year 2014, and to Amend the First Paragraph of Article 2 of the Federal Revenue Act for Fiscal Year 2013], art. 1, D.O., Nov. 20, 2013.

[447] *El 2014 Inicia con Nuevos Impuestos; Gasolina, Pan, Comida, Chatarra y Para Mascotas ya Tienen Carga Fiscal*, SINEMBARGO.MX (Jan. 1, 2014), http://www.sinembargo.mx/01-01-2014/859905.

[448] Ing. Arturo M. Monforte Ocampo, Conservación de Carreteras Federales Libres de Peaje 10–11 (Academia de Ingienería, A.C. 2008), http://www.ai.org.mx/ai/ (click on "Eventos Y Publicaciones," then "Coloquios," then "VI," and then, under "Ing. Arturo Manuel Monforte Ocampo," click on "Descargar Trabajo").

[449] *Inland Transport Infrastructure at Regional Level*, European Commission/Eurostat (Dec. 2010), http://epp.eurostat.ec.europa.eu/statistics_explained/index.php/Inland_transport_infrastructure_at_regional_level.

[450] Tomasz Kozluk, *How the Transport System Can Contribute to Better Economic and Environmental Outcomes in the Netherlands* 12 (OECD Economics Department, Working Paper No. 804, Oct. 6, 2010), http://dx.doi.org/10.1787/5km68g0zh7ls-en (click on "PDF").

[451] *Id.*, citing to L. Molenkamp, PowerPoint Presentation, *Traffic Congestion – The Netherlands' Approach*, Ministry of Transport, Public Works and Water Management, Rijkswaterstaat (London, July 2007).

[452] *Welkom op Autosnelwegen.nl* [*Welcome to Autosnelwegen.nl*], Autosnelwegen.nl, http://www.autosnelwegen.nl/. This website "is dedicated to the history of Dutch national roads system in general, and motorways in particular" and is not part of the Rijkswaterstaat, which administers the highway network. *Id.* For a map of the system, see Rijkswaterstaat, http://www.rijkswaterstaat.nl/en/images/main-highway-network_tcm224-340839.jpg (last visited Feb. 20, 2014).

[453] *Welkom op Autosnelwegen.nl*, *supra* note 4.

[454] *About Us*, Rijkswaterstaat, http://www.rijkswaterstaat.nl/en/about_us/ (last visited Feb. 20, 2014).

[455] *Wegbeheer in Nederland* [*Road Management in the Netherlands*], Rijkswaterstaat, http://www.rijkswaterstaat. nl/wegen/feiten_en_cijfers/wegbeheer/ (last visited Feb. 27, 2014).

[456] Grondwet voor het Koninkrijk der Nederlanden van 24 augustus 1815 [Constitution of the Kingdom of the Netherlands of 24 August 1815] (last amended June 27, 2008, in force on July 15, 2008), available on the official government website Overheid.nl, *at* http://wetten.overheid.nl/BWBR0001840/geldigheidsdatum_05-02-2014; for an English translation, see The Constitution of the Kingdom of the Netherlands 2008 art. 105(4), http://www.rijksoverheid.nl/documenten-en-publicaties/brochures/2008/10/20/the-constitution-of-the- kingdom-of-the-netherlands-2008.html.

[457] *Id.* art. 104.

[458] *Id.* art. 105.

[459] *Id.* art. 132(6).

[460] *Id.* art. 124(1 & 2).

[461] Wet bereikbaarheid en mobiliteit [Law on Accessibility and Mobility] (July 4, 2002, as last amended effective Jan. 1, 2013), art. 10 1, http://wetten.overheid.nl/BWBR0013854/geldigheidsdatum_21-02-2014.

[462] *Id.* art. 4 1.

[463] *Id.* art. 4 2.

[464] *Id.* arts. 15 1 & 21 1.

[465] *Id.* art. 21 2.

[466] *Id.* art. 21 3. This provision refers to the respective sections of the tax laws concerned, i.e., ch. XV of the Provinciewet, §§ 1 & 4 of ch. XV of the Gemeentewet, and chs. XVI & XVIII of the Waterschapswet.

[467] Wet Infrastructuurfonds [Infrastructure Fund Act] (May 27, 1993, as last amended effective Jan. 1, 2012), art. 2 2a, http://wetten.overheid.nl/BWBR0006001/geldigheidsdatum_21-02-2014.

[468] *Id.* art. 2 2b.

[469] Jordy van Meerkerk, Gusta Renes & Geert Ridder, *Greening the Dutch Car Fleet: The Role of Differentiated Sales Taxes* (PBL Netherlands Environmental Assessment Agency, Working Paper No. 18, Jan. 2014), http://www.pbl.nl/en/publications/greening-the-dutch-car-fleet-

the-role-of-differentiated-sales-taxes (click on "download the working paper"). The authors provide a table of selected pretax prices (net list-price), the value, and the rate of the vehicle sales tax in the Netherlands for 2005 (before the new system began) and 2010.

470 *Vehicle Taxes*, GOVERNMENT OF THE NETHERLANDS, http://government.nl/issues/taxation/vehicle-taxes (last visited Feb. 24, 2014); Wet op de belasting op personenauto's en motorrijwielen 1992 [Passenger Car and Motorcycles Tax Act 1992] (Dec. 24, 1992, as last amended effective Jan. 1, 2014), http://wetten.overheid.nl/BWBR0005806/geldigheidsdatum_24-02-2014.

471 Passenger Car and Motorcycles Tax Act 1992 arts. 9–12.

472 *VEHICLE TAXES*, *SUPRA* NOTE 22; WET OP DE MOTORRIJTUIGENBELASTING 1994 [MOTOR VEHICLE TAX ACT 1994] (DEC. 16, 1993, AS LAST AMENDED EFFECTIVE JAN. 1, 2014), HTTP://WETTEN.OVERHEID.NL/BWBR0006324/GELDIGHEIDSDATUM_24-02-2014.

473 *Vehicle Taxes*, *supra* note 22.

474 Motor Vehicle Tax Act 1994 arts. 22–32.

475 *Id. See also Taxation of Heavy Goods Vehicles: Eurovignette Directive*, EUROPA, http://europa.eu/legislation_summaries/internal_market/single_market_for_goods/motor_vehicles/interactions_industry_policies/l24045b_en.ht m (last updated Oct. 13, 2008).

476 Wet op de accijns [Law on Excise Duty] (Oct. 31, 1991, as last amended effective Jan. 1, 2014), arts. 26–27, http://wetten.overheid.nl/BWBR0005251/geldigheidsdatum_04-01-2014.

477 *Netherlands - VAT Rates Table* (effective rates Mar. 1, 2013) (last reviewed Sept. 1, 2013), International Bureau of Fiscal Documentation online subscription database, http://online.ibfd.org/kbase/#topic=doc&url=%252Fcollections%252Fvatrates%252Fhtml%252Fvatrates_nl.html&q=fuel+tax+fuels+taxes&WT.z_nav=outline&colid=4929&hash=vatrates_nl.

478 *See, e.g.*, Kozluk, *supra* note 2; Ministerie van Verkeer en Waterstaat [Ministry of Transport, Public Works and Water Management], PowerPoint Presentation, *Road Pricing in the Netherlands: Overview* (Jan. 13, 2010), http://www.internationaltransportforum.org/jtrc/RoundTables/RTfeb10vanWortel.pdf; MINISTER OF TRANSPORT, PUBLIC WORKS AND WATER MANAGEMENT, RULES FOR CHARGING A PAY-BY-USE PRICE FOR DRIVING WITH A MOTOR VEHICLE [DUTCH ROAD PRICING ACT] (undated), http://i95coalition.org/i95/Portals/0/Public_Files/pm/ reports/Netherlands%20Road%20Pricing%20Study.pdf.

479 The package of measures comprised the Bereikbaarheidsoffensief Randstad [Accessibility Offensive Randstad], the Randstad being a conurbation of Amsterdam, Rotterdam, The Hague, and Utrecht and their surrounding areas. *OECD Territorial Reviews: Randstad Holland, Netherlands*, OECD), http://www.oecd.org/netherlands/oecd territorialreviewsrandstadhollandnetherlands.htm (last visited Feb. 28. 2014).

480 Eduard Scheenstra, *The Netherlands*, *in* PPP IN EUROPE 81 (Aug. 2010), http://www.cmslegal.cn/Hubbard.File System/files/Publication/ed219c67-c7b1-40c6-a54d-3494ef81e6c8/Presentation/PublicationAttachment/33ec4891-c549-49f4-b161-370b851fbd78/CMS_PPPinEurope_Guide082010.pdf.

481 Thao Hua, *British, Dutch Forge Path for Infrastructure Investing: Government-Backed Initiatives Ease Way for Pension Funds to Invest in Asset Class*, PENSIONS & INVESTMENTS (Sept. 17, 2012), http://www.pionline.com/article/20120917/PRINT/309179984/british-dutch-forge-paths-for-infrastructure-investing.

482 MARK COBLEY, *DUTCH FUNDS DISAPPOINTED BY GOVERNMENT'S INFRASTRUCTURE PULLOUT* (JUNE 12, 2013), HTTP://WWW.EFINANCIALNEWS.COM/STORY/2013-06-12/DUTCH-FUNDS- UNPLEASANTLY-SURPRISED-GOVERNMENT-INFRASTRUCTURE.

483 *Linklaters Advises on Major Dutch Roads Project - A1/A6*, LINKLATERS (Feb. 17, 2013), http://www.linklaters. com/News/LatestDeals/2013/Pages/Linklaters-advises-major-Dutch-roads-project-A1A6.aspx.

[484] Directive 2010/40/EU of the European Parliament and of the Council of 7 July 2010 on the Framework for the Deployment of Intelligent Transport Systems in the Field of Road Transport and for Interfaces with Other Modes of Transport, 2010 O.J. (L 207/1), http://eur-lex.europa.eu/LexUriServ/LexUriServ.do?uri=OJ:L:2010:207:0001:0013:EN:PDF.

[485] MINISTRY OF INFRASTRUCTURE AND THE ENVIRONMENT, ITS-PLAN THE NETHERLANDS: 2013–2017 16 (2012), http://ec.europa.eu/transport/themes/its/road/action_plan/doc/2012-its-plan-the-netherlands-2013-2017.pdf.

[486] *Id.*

[487] *Id.*

[488] S. AFR. CONST. § 40(1), 1996, http://www.info.gov.za/documents/ constitution/1996/ index.htm.

[489] *Id.* sched. 4.

[490] *Id.* sched. 5.

[491] *Id.* § 44(1). Pursuant to Section 44 (2), the national government legislates on such matters when it is necessary

a. to maintain national security;
b. to maintain economic unity;
c. to maintain essential national standards;
d. to establish minimum standards required for the rendering of services; or
e. to prevent unreasonable action taken by a province which is prejudicial to the interests of another province or to the country as a whole.

[492] Marvyn Dendy, *Roads and Road Transport*, *in* 23 THE LAWS OF SOUTH AFRICA (W.A. Joubert et al. eds., 2d ed. 2009).

[493] South African National Roads Agency Limited and National Roads Act No. 7 of 1998, 31(1) BUTTERWORTHS STATUTES OF THE REPUBLIC OF SOUTH AFRICA (*rev'd.* through 2012).

[494] *Id.* § 1.

[495] *Id.* § 40.

[496] *Id.*

[497] *Id.*

[498] *Id.*

[499] *Id.* § 2.

[500] *Id.* § 3.

[501] *Id.* § 12; *Overview*, SANRAL, http://www.nra.co.za/live/content.php?Item_ID=151 (last visited Jan. 22, 2014).

[502] South African National Roads Agency Limited and National Roads Act § 25.

[503] *Id.* § 26.

[504] *Id.*

[505] *Id.*

[506] *Id.*

[507] *Id.*

[508] A fuel levy is imposed under the Customs and Excise Act No. 91 of 1964, § 47, 10 BUTTERWORTHS STATUTES OF THE REPUBLIC OF SOUTH AFRICA (*rev'd.* through 2012). The levy goes into the country's National Revenue Fund (NRF) and it does not appear to be earmarked specifically for infrastructure spending. The NRF is a fund "into which all money received by the national government must be paid, except money reasonably excluded by an act of Parliament." (S. AFR. CONST. § 213.) There are two ways of withdrawing money from the NRF: through parliamentary appropriations; or as a direct charge against the [NRF] if mandated by the Constitution or an Act of Parliament. (*Id.*)

[509] South African National Roads Agency Limited and National Roads Act § 34.

[510] *Id.* § 26; *Finance*, SANRAL, http://www.nra.co.za/live/content.php? Category_ID=29 (last visited Jan. 22, 2014).

[511] SANRAL, ANNUAL REPORT 2013, at 26 (undated), http://sanral.ensight-cdn.com/ content/Sanral_Annual_ Report_13_LRES.pdf.

[512] SANRAL, STRATEGIC PLAN 2012/2013–2016/2017, at 7 (undated), http://www.nra.co.za/live/click.php?u=//sanral.ensight-cdn.com/content/Strategic_Plan2012_13_2016_17%7E1.pdf&o=Item%2B4582&v=1ba306.

[513] SOUTH AFRICAN NATIONAL ROADS AGENCY SOC LTD. OPERATING SUMMARY (NON TOLL) BUDGET (undated), http://sanral.ensight-cdn.com/content/Non_Toll_Budget_Summary_Page_2012_2013~1.pdf.

[514] *Id.*

[515] SANRAL, STRATEGIC PLAN, *supra* note 25, at 7.

[516] STRATEGIC VISION OF THE SOUTH AFRICAN NATIONAL ROADS AGENCY FOR THE YEAR 2010, at 25 (2004), http://www.nra.co.za/content/horizon2010.pdf.

[517] SANRAL, STRATEGIC PLAN, *supra* note 25, at 14.

[518] *Id.*

[519] South African National Roads Agency Limited and National Roads Act § 27.

[520] *Id.*

[521] *Id.* §§ 27 & 28.

[522] *Id.* § 28.

[523] SANRAL, STRATEGIC PLAN, *supra* note 25, at 7.

[524] *Id.* at 53.

[525] *Id.*

[526] *Finance*, SANRAL, *supra* note 23; South African National Roads Agency Limited and National Roads Act § 33.

[527] SANRAL, STRATEGIC PLAN, *supra* note 25, at 53.

[528] SANRAL, ANNUAL REPORT, *supra* note 24, at 121.

[529] SANRAL, STRATEGIC PLAN, *supra* note 25, at 53.

[530] SANRAL, ANNUAL REPORT, *supra* note 24, at 121.

[531] *Id.*

[532] *Id.* at 121 & 147; SANRAL, STRATEGIC PLAN, *supra* note 25, at 54.

[533] SANRAL, ANNUAL REPORT, *supra* note 24, at 121 & 147.

[534] SANRAL, STRATEGIC PLAN, *supra* note 25, at 14.

[535] *Id.*

[536] *Id.* at 52.

[537] SANRAL, ANNUAL REPORT, *supra* note 24, at 35.

[538] 11 § VÄGLAG (Svensk Författningssamling [SFS] 1971:948), http://www.notisum.se/rnp/sls/lag/19710948.htm. If these agencies cannot agree then the issue is sent to the government for review.

[539] *Id* § 14b.

[540] *Id.*

[541] ALF BOHLIN, KOMMUNALRÄTTENS GRUNDER 136–37 (6th ed. 2011).

[542] *Id.*

[543] TRAFIKVERKET, FÖRSLAG TILL NATIONELL PLAN (Oct. 18, 2013), http://www.trafikverket.se/Foretag/Planera-och-utreda/Planer-och-beslutsunderlag/Nationell-planering/Nationell-plan-for-transportsystemet-2014--2025/Forslag- till-Nationell-plan/.

[544] GUNNAR MALM, GENERALDIRECTÖR, TRAFIKVERKET, NATIONELL TRANSPORTPLAN 2014–2025 (June 14, 2013), http://www.trafikverket.se/PageFiles/129095/presentation_14_juni_forslag_nationell_transportplan.pdf.

[545] *Sveriges vägnät*, TRAFIKVERKET, http://www.trafikverket.se/Privat/Vagar-och-jarnvagar/Sveriges-vagnat/ (last updated Jan. 23, 2014).

[546] *Id.*

[547] *See* Statens Offentliga Utredningar [SOU] 2004:63 Skatt på väg, at 221, http://www.regeringen.se/sb/d/108/a/24111 (government report series).

[548] Proposition [Prop.] 2005/06:65 Ny trafikskattelag m.m. at 70, http://www.regeringen.se/sb/d/5019/a/55391 (government bill).

549 VÄGTRAFFIKSKATTELAG (SFS 2006:227), http://www.riksdagen.se/sv/Dokument-Lagar/ Lagar/ Svensk forfattningssamling/ Vagtrafikskattelag-2006227_sfs-2006-227/.

550 LAG MED SÄRSKILDA BESTÄMMELSER OM FORDONSSKATT (SFS 2006:228), http://www.notisum.se/rnp/sls/lag/20060228.htm.

551 2 ch. 9 § VÄGTRAFIKSKATTELAG.

552 *Id.*

553 *Id.* 10 §.

554 *See id.*

555 11 § VÄGSKATTELAGEN. For a historical background on the motor vehicle tax, which was previously only based on a car's weight, see Prop. 2005/06:65 Ny vägtrafikskattelag, m.m. at 64, http://www.regeringen.se/sb/d/5019/a/55391.

556 *Trängselskatt i Stockholm*, TRANSPORTSTYRELSEN, http://www.transportstyrelsen.se/Vag/ Trangselskatt/Trangselskatt-i-stockholm/ (last modified Jan. 8, 2014).

557 *Trängselskatt i Göteborg*, TRANSPORTSTYRELSEN, http://www.transportstyrelsen.se/sv/ Vag/ Trangselskatt/ Trangselskatt-i-goteborg/ (last modified Jan. 8, 2014).

558 LAG OM TRÄNGSELSKATT (SFS 2004:629), http://www.riksdagen.se/sv/Dokument-Lagar/Lagar/ Svensk forfattningssamling/Lag-2004629-om-trangselskat_sfs-2004-629/.

559 *Id.* 1 §.

560 *Trängselskatt i Stockholm*, TRANSPORTSTYRELSEN, *supra* note 19.

561 Prop. 2003/04:145, TRÄNGSELSKATT at 23.

562 *Id.* at 35.

563 *Id.*

564 *Trängselskatt i Stockholm*, TRANSPORTSTYRELSEN, *supra* note 19.

565 *Id.*

566 Prop. 2003/04:145 at 24.

567 *Id.* at 23–26.

568 *Id.*

569 *Svinesundförbindelsen*, TRANSPORTSTYRELSEN (May 5, 2010), http://www.transportstyrelsen. se/sv/Vag/ Fordon/Vagavgifter/Vagavgifter-i-Sverige/ Svinesundsforbindelsen/ (last updated Dec. 10, 2013); *Vägavgift vid Svinesund*, SVINESUNFORBINDELSEN AS, http://www.svinesundsforbindelsen.no/svensk/svinesund.htm (last visited Feb. 7, 2014).

570 2 § FÖRORDNING OM AVGIFT FÖR FÄRD PÅ SVINESUNDSFÖRBINDELSEN (SFS 2005:531), http://www.riksdagen. se/sv/Dokument-Lagar/Lagar/Svenskforfattningssamling/Forordning -2005531-om-avgif_sfs-2005-531/.

571 *Id.* 2 § st. 2.

572 *Id.* 5 §.

573 *Id.* 6 §.

574 LAG OM SKATT PÅ ENERGI (SFS 1994:1776), http://www.riksdagen.se/sv/Dokument-Lagar/ Lagar/Svensk forfattningssamling/sfs_sfs-1994-1776/.

575 *Id.* ch. 2:1 §.

576 *Id.*

577 *Så här byggs bensinpriset upp*, PREEM, http://www.preem.se/templates/page 791.aspx (last visited Jan. 17, 2014).

578 *Vill medfinansiera E20-utbyggnad*, VÄSTRA GÖTALANDSREGIONEN, http://www. vgregion.se/ sv/Vastra-Gotalandsregionen/startsida/Om-Vastra-Gotalandsregionen/Nyheter/ Aktuella-nyheter/ Vill-medfinansiera-E20- utbyggnad/ (last updated June 7, 2013).

579 Ulf Nyström, *Regionstrid om utbyggnad på E20*, GP (Apr. 10, 2012; updated Apr. 11, 2012), http://www.gp.se/nyheter/goteborg/1.911834-regionstrid-om-utbyggnad-pa-e20.

580 *Förbifart Stockholm*, TRAFIKVERKET, http://www.trafikverket.se/forbifartstockholm (last updated Jan. 14, 2014).

581 SOU 2013:84 Fossilfritt på väg, http://www.regeringen.se/sb/d/17075/a/230739.

582 *Id.* at 628.

[583] *Id.*; *see also Vägavgifter i Sverige*, TRANSPORTSTYRELSEN, http://www. transportstyrelsen.se/ sv/Vag/Fordon/Vagavgifter/Vagavgifter-i-Sverige/ (last modified May 5, 2010).

In: Road Infrastructure Funding
Editor: Russell T. May
ISBN: 978-1-63321-633-4

Chapter 2

FUNDING AND FINANCING HIGHWAYS AND PUBLIC TRANSPORTATION*

Robert S. Kirk and William J. Mallett

SUMMARY

Federal surface transportation programs are currently funded primarily through taxes on motor fuels that are deposited in the highway trust fund (HTF). Although there has been some modification to the tax system, the tax rates, which are fixed in terms of cents per gallon, have not been increased at the federal level since 1993. Prior to the recession that began in 2007, annual increases in driving, with a concomitant increase in fuel use, were sufficient to keep revenues rising steadily. This is no longer the case. Future increases in fuel economy standards are expected to suppress motor fuel consumption in the years ahead even if annual increases in vehicle mileage resume.

Congress has yet to address the surface transportation program's fundamental revenue issues, and has given limited legislative consideration to raising fuel taxes in recent years. Instead, Congress has financed the federal surface transportation program by supplementing fuel tax revenues with transfers from the U.S. Treasury general fund. The most recent reauthorization act, the Moving Ahead for Progress in the 21st Century Act (MAP-21; P.L. 112-141), signed by President Barack Obama on July 6, 2012, authorized spending on federal highway and

* This is an edited, reformatted and augmented version of a Congressional Research Service publication, No. R42877, dated April 4, 2014.

public transportation programs through September 30, 2014, and provided for general fund transfers to finance the programs. MAP-21 did not address concerns about funding of surface transportation programs over the longer term.

This report begins with a discussion of the challenges facing the trust fund financing system (which supports both federal highway and public transportation programs) and then explores possible options for financing surface transportation infrastructure. Among the key points:

- Raising motor fuel taxes could provide the HTF with sufficient revenue to fully fund the program in the near term, but it may not be a viable long-term solution due to expected future declines in fuel consumption.
- Replacing current motor fuel taxes with a fuel sales tax or a fee based on vehicle miles traveled (VMT) raise a variety of financial and administrative concerns.
- Treasury general fund transfers could be used to make up for the HTF's projected shortfalls but would require budget offsets of an equal amount, as required by the January 2014 budget resolution (H.Con.Res. 25, §608).
- The political difficulty of adequately financing the HTF could lead Congress to consider the desirability of changes to maintain the trust fund system or of eliminating it altogether. Such changes might involve a reallocation of responsibilities and obligations among federal, state, and local governments.
- Interest in improving transportation infrastructure with private and non-grant funding sources, such as tolls, public-private partnerships (P3s), and federal loan programs, is increasing, but many projects may not be well suited to alternative financing.

INTRODUCTION

Almost every conversation about surface transportation finance begins with a two-part question: what are the "needs" of the national transportation system and how does the nation pay for them? This report is aimed almost entirely at discussing the "how to pay for them" question. Since 1956, federal surface transportation programs have been funded largely by taxes on motor fuels that flow into the highway trust fund (HTF). A steady increase in the revenues flowing into the HTF, due to increased motor vehicle use and occasional increases in federal fuel taxes, has accommodated growth in surface transportation spending over several decades. The growth in trust fund revenues, however, came to an end in 2008. Over the past six years there has been a large gap between the dedicated revenues flowing into the HTF and funding of surface transportation authorized by Congress.

This gap was not totally unexpected. The authors of the Safe, Accountable, Flexible, Efficient Transportation Equity Act: A Legacy for Users (SAFETEA, FY2005-FY2009; P.L. 109-59) set up two commissions to advise Congress on changes to the surface transportation program and its funding mechanisms. To date, however, Congress has made no major changes in transportation financing, aside from authorizing transfers of money from the Treasury general fund to the HTF.

The Moving Ahead for Progress in the 21st Century Act (MAP-21; P.L. 112-141), signed July 6, 2012,[1] authorized spending on federal highway and public transportation programs through September 30, 2014, and provided for extensive transfers from the general fund to the HTF. The mismatch between the desired surface transportation program and the revenues generated by motor fuel taxes persists, and may emerge as a major issue as Congress considers options for reauthorizing the program beyond 2014.

THE HIGHWAY TRUST FUND FINANCING DILEMMA

The highway trust fund has two separate accounts—highways and mass transit. The primary revenue sources for these accounts are an 18.4-cent-per-gallon federal tax on gasoline and a 24.4- cent-per-gallon federal tax on diesel fuel. Although the HTF has other sources of revenue, such as truck registration fees and a truck tire tax, and is also credited with interest paid on the fund balances held by the U.S. Treasury, fuel taxes provide about 90% of the income to the fund. The transit account receives 2.86 cents per gallon of fuel taxes, with the remainder of the tax revenue flowing into the highway account. Separately, there is a 0.1-cent-per-gallon fuel tax reserved for the leaking underground storage tank (LUST) fund, which is not part of the transportation program.

Since the trust fund was created in 1956, motor fuel taxes have increased four times, in 1959, 1982, 1990, and 1993. The last two increases were initially partially reserved for deficit reduction purposes, with significant sums being deposited in the Treasury general fund account. By FY1998, following several years of congressional debate, all fuel tax collections were again being deposited into the trust fund.

Since the 1993 tax increase, additional changes to the taxation structure have modestly increased trust fund revenues. The American Jobs Creation Act of 2004 (P.L. 108-357), for example, provided the trust fund with increased future income by changing elements of federal "gasohol" taxation. In 2005, the finance title of SAFETEA included a number of tax and other revenue-raising changes designed to bolster the trust fund, mainly by addressing tax fraud. SAFETEA also provided for the transfer of some general fund revenues associated with transportation-related activities to the trust fund. It was believed at the time of SAFETEA's passage that the tax changes, a $12.5 billion unexpended balance in the trust fund, and, most important, expected economic growth would be sufficient to finance the program through its expiration at the end of FY2009.[2] This prediction proved to be incorrect.

The shortfalls resulting from the overly optimistic forecasts associated with SAFETEA were rectified by Treasury general fund contributions. Congress directed an $8 billion transfer from the general fund to the highway account in FY2008 (P.L. 110-318). In FY2009, it provided for a $7 billion transfer (P.L. 111-46). In FY2010, the Hiring Incentives to Restore Employment (HIRE) Act (P.L. 111-147) provided $14.7 billion in general fund monies to the highway account and, for the first time, a general fund transfer of $4.8 billion to the transit account.

The era of automatic trust fund growth may be over, because annual vehicle miles traveled (VMT) are no longer increasing at the 2% average rate experienced from 1960s until 2008. The main immediate cause of stagnation in VMT is the sluggish economy, which has suppressed growth in personal incomes (reducing leisure travel), reduced work-related driving, and also weakened demand for freight shipments. Over the longer term, other forces are putting pressure on the trust fund mechanism. Most important, recent policy changes are weakening the link between driving activity and motor fuel tax revenues. On August 28, 2012, the Obama Administration issued new passenger vehicle fuel economy standards for vehicle model years 2017-2025. Under these standards combined new passenger car and light truck Corporate Average Fuel Economy (CAFE) standards are expected to rise to as high as 41.0 miles per gallon in model year 2021 and 49.7 miles per gallon in model year 2025, thus reducing the outlook for the number of gallons of fuel used.[3] Meanwhile, the expanding fleet of hybrid and electric vehicles will, respectively, pay less or nothing by way of fuel taxes.[4]

An increase in the existing fuel tax rates would provide immediate relief to the trust fund. As a rule of thumb, adding a penny to federal motor fuel taxes provides the trust fund with roughly $1.5 billion per year.[5] The prospect of reduced motor fuel consumption, however, casts doubt on the ability of the motor fuel taxes to support increased surface transportation spending beyond the next decade even with modest increases in tax rates. [6] In considering reauthorization of MAP-21, Congress could face a choice between finding new sources of income for the surface transportation program and settling for a smaller program, which might look very different from the one currently in place.

MAP-21 provided for general fund transfers of $6.2 billion and $12.6 billion for FY2013 and FY2014, respectively.[7] Also, $2.4 billion of the accrued balance of the LUST fund was transferred to the HTF for FY2012. Even so, according to Congressional Budget Office (CBO) estimates, the highway account of the HTF will retain a balance of only $1 billion at the expiration of MAP-21 in September 2014, far below the $4 billion level cash amount considered prudent. [8] As a result, the highway account could have to delay some payments near the end of FY2014. The mass transit account is expected to have a balance of $2 billion at that time.

What Congress Faces

According to projections by the CBO, revenue flowing into the HTF through 2020 pursuant to existing law will fall far short of the amount needed to sustain the current level of outlays (see **Table 1**). CBO projects that HTF revenues will fall short of outlays by an average of about $16 billion per year, or $95 billion over a six-year period. Although the HTF cannot run negative balances under current law, CBO projects a cumulative shortfall in both accounts combined starting in FY2015, meaning the HTF would not have the money available to reimburse state governments and local transit agencies in a timely fashion. The total shortfall over the six years would be $100 billion if the bill were to include a provision for maintenance of a $5 billion "prudent balance" in the HTF to assure its ability to pay bills as they are presented.[9] This is what the House Ways and Means Committee and the Senate Committee on Finance face in terms of raising revenues or finding offsets for Treasury general fund transfers, should Congress choose to fund surface transportation at the current, or "baseline," level, adjusted for inflation.

Table 1. Projected HTF Sufficiency: FY2015-FY2020
Billions of Dollars

Fiscal Year	HTF Revenue	Obligations Amount	Obligations Difference	HTF Outlays Amount	HTF Outlays Difference
2015	$39	$52	$-13	$54	$-15
2016	39	52	-14	54	-15
2017	39	54	-15	54	-15
2018	39	55	-16	55	-16
2019	39	56	-17	56	-17
2020	39	57	-18	56	-17
4-YR: FY2015-2018 Total	156	213	-58	217	-61
4-YR: FY2015-2018 Average	39	53	-15	54	-15
6-YR: FY2015-2020 Total	234	326	-92	329	-95
6-YR: FY2015-2020 Average	39	54	-15	55	-16

Source: CRS calculations based on CBO, *Highway Trust Fund Projections: February 2014 HTF Baseline 2013-2024.* HTF obligations are obligation limitations plus annual exempt obligations. Figures may not add due to rounding.

Notes: Includes combined figures from both the highway account and the mass transit account. Obligations do not reflect Federal Transit Administration general fund authorizations. The "HTF Revenue" column includes interest on the HTF balances.

Since the HTF currently provides all but about $2 billion of annual spending authorized in the surface transportation act (the main exception being the Federal Transit Administration's (FTA's) New Starts program), these numbers have implications for the size of the program Congress can approve. Shaping a program that could be supported by revenues that now flow into the HTF implies annual highway and transit outlays of roughly $39 billion through 2020, significantly less than FY2014 outlays of roughly $54 billion.[10] It also implies that the Federal Highway Administration (FHWA) and FTA would have less contract authority to approve projects on which money would be spent in future years.[11]

The center columns in **Table 1** project the annual amount of funds the federal government could obligate (promise to pay) from the trust fund given the revenues and outlays shown in the table. These are the approximate funds available for obligation that the authorizing committees would have available to work with within a baseline-plus-inflation surface transportation bill.

Under this scenario, total obligation limitations, exempt obligations plus projected Treasury general funds for FTA (roughly $2 billion per year), would add to a four-year bill total of roughly $221 billion and a six-year total of roughly $339 billion. This would be for a baseline-plusinflation bill with no net increase in the program size.[12]

A smaller program might not provide immediate relief from the demands on the HTF. Because of the multiyear nature of the highway and public transportation programs and the multiyear availability of the contract authority that supports them, both programs have ongoing existing commitments. For FY2014, unspent contract authority for highway programs is expected to total roughly $66 billion in unpaid obligated balances and $25 billion in unobligated contract authority. For the public transportation programs these figures are roughly $14 billion in unpaid obligations and $10 billion in unobligated contract authority.[13] These obligations have been incurred by the federal government (under binding agreements such as highway project agreements) and must be paid.[14]

EXISTING HIGHWAY FUEL TAXES[15]

The first federal tax on gasoline (1 cent per gallon) was imposed in 1932, during the Hoover Administration, as a deficit-reduction measure following the depression-induced fall in general revenues. The rate was raised to help pay for World War II (to 1.5 cents per gallon) and raised again during the Korean War (to 2 cents per gallon). The rate was raised in 1956 (to 3 cents per gallon) and 1959 (to 4 cents per gallon) to establish the HTF and fund it to pay for the construction of the Interstate Highway system. The gasoline tax remained at 4 cents from October 1, 1959, until March 31, 1983.

One of the attractive attributes of highway fuel taxes to policy makers during much of the history of the HTF was that revenues grew automatically from year to year, so long as vehicle miles traveled grew. Despite this, since 1983 lawmakers have passed legislation raising the tax rates on highway fuel use three times. Although infrequent, these rate increases were quite large in a proportional sense.

The gasoline tax was raised on April 1, 1983, from 4 to 9 cents per gallon, a 125% increase; on September 1, 1990, from 9 to 14 (not counting the additional 0.1 cent for LUST), or 55%, and on October 1, 1993, from 14 to 18.3 cents, or 31%.[16]

How the Rates Have Been Raised Since 1983

Increasing the rate of the fuel taxes has never been popular. The last three increases were accomplished with difficulty and were influenced by the broader budgetary environment and the practical politics of the time.[17]

The "Great Compromise" and the Highway "User Fee," the Surface Transportation Assistance Act of 1982 (STAA; P.L. 97-424, Title V)

The increase in the fuel tax rate under STAA occurred in the lame-duck session of the 97th Congress. In the Great Compromise, supporters of increased highway spending had come to an agreement with transit supporters (mostly from the Northeast) that a penny of a proposed 5-centsper-gallon increase would be dedicated to a new mass transit account within the HTF. This meant that support for the bill during the lame-duck session was widespread and bipartisan. During the congressional elections of 1982 the Democrats had picked up 26 seats in the House of Representatives. The economy was experiencing a major recession and some argued that increased highway spending would stimulate the economy. President Reagan's opposition to an increase in the "gas tax" softened during the lame-duck session. On November 23, 1982, President Reagan announced that he would support passage of STAA, even though it would "mean an increase in the highway user fee, or gas tax, of 5 cents a gallon ... Our country's outstanding highway system was built on the user fee principle—that those who benefit from a use should share in its cost."[18] Nonetheless, the bill faced a series of filibusters in the Senate, which were eventually overcome by four cloture votes. The conference report was again filibustered, and President Reagan helped secure the votes needed for cloture. President Reagan signed STAA into law on January 6, 1983, more than doubling the highway fuel tax to 9 cents per gallon.

50/50 Share: Deficit Reduction/Highway Trust Fund; the Omnibus Budget Reconciliation Act of 1990 (OBRA90; P.L. 101-508)

OBRA90, enacted November 5, 1990, was passed under the pressure of impending final FY1991 sequestration orders issued by President George H. W. Bush under Title II of P.L. 99-177, the Balanced Budget and Emergency Deficit Control Act of 1985, known as the Gramm-Rudman-Hollings Act (GRH). OBRA90 included budget cuts, tax changes, and the Budget Enforcement Act (P.L. 101-508), which rescinded the FY1991 sequestration orders. OBRA90 also raised the tax on gasoline by 5 cents per gallon to 14 cents. Half the increase went to the HTF (2 cents to the highway account and 0.5 cents to the mass transit account), with the other 2.5 cents per gallon to be deposited in the general fund for deficit reduction. This was the first time since 1957 the motor fuel tax had been used as a source of general revenue. Section 9001 expressed the sense of Congress that all motor fuel taxes should be directed to the HTF as soon as possible.

More for Deficit Reduction; the Omnibus Budget Reconciliation Act of 1993 (OBRA93; P.L. 103-66)

OBRA93 Section 13241(a) made further changes in regard to fuel taxes:

- The 2.5-cents-per-gallon fuel tax dedicated to deficit reduction in OBRA90 was redirected to the HTF beginning October 1, 1995, and its authorization was extended to September 30, 1999.
- The highway account received 2 cents per gallon and the mass transit account 0.5 cents per gallon of the rededicated amount.
- An additional permanent 4.3 cents per gallon fuel tax took effect in October 1993 and was dedicated to deficit reduction.

This brought the gasoline tax to 18.3 cents per gallon, although for two years (October 1, 1993, to October 1, 1995) 6.8 cents per gallon of this was deposited in the general fund, dedicated to deficit reduction. On October 1, 1995, the amount going to the general fund dropped to 4.3 cents per gallon and the amount dedicated to the HTF increased to 14 cents per gallon.

Subsequently, under the Taxpayer Relief Act of 1997 (P.L. 105-34), all motor fuel tax revenue was redirected to the HTF (3.45 cents to the highway account and 0.85 cents to the mass transit account), effective October 1, 1997. (The LUST fund continues to receive the revenue from an additional 0.1 cents per gallon tax.)

Since that time, revenue flowing into the HTF has not met expectations in most years, and has generally lagged inflation since FY2007.[19] In some years, HTF revenue has declined even in nominal terms due to reduced vehicle travel. Because of the fixed nature of the cents-per-gallon gasoline and diesel taxes, the only way the taxes can generate additional revenue for the HTF is if motor-fuel consumption rises.[20] However, according to the Energy Information Administration, retail gasoline sales declined for five consecutive years before rising in 2013, and diesel fuel use by highway vehicles peaked in 2007.[21]

Alternatives for HTF Financing

The political difficulty of increasing motor fuel taxes has led to interest in alternative approaches for supporting the HTF. These involve tying motor fuel tax rates to the price of fuel, changing the structure of the current fuel taxes, and charging drivers for the distance they drive rather than the fuel they consume, as well as freight-related charges and a variety of nontransportation-related options. Revenue estimates by AASHTO for many such proposals are provided in **Figure 1**.

Sales Taxes

Under the sales tax concept, the federal motor fuel tax would be assessed as a percentage of the retail price of fuel rather than as a fixed amount per gallon. Some states already levy taxes on motor fuels in this way, either alongside or in place of fixed cents-per-gallon taxes on motor fuel purchases.

The American Association of State Highway and Transportation Officials (AASHTO) estimates for 2015-2020 that an 8.0% tax on gasoline sales and an 11% tax on diesel sales would together average roughly $47 billion in revenues each year, roughly $8 billion over CBO's projected annual HTF revenues and interest. If fuel prices rise in the future, sales tax revenues could rise from year to year even if consumption does not increase. The sales tax rates could be adjusted in future years, if necessary, to keep up with inflation in construction costs.

Conversely, however, a decline in motor fuels prices could lead to a drop in sales tax revenue. Many states that tied fuel taxes to prices after the price shocks of the 1970s encountered revenue shortfalls in the 1980s, when fuel prices fell dramatically. Over a 20-year period, most of these variable state fuel taxes disappeared.[22] Recently, however, Virginia eliminated its cents-per-gallon fuel taxes in favor of a sales tax on fuel and a general sales tax increase that was dedicated to transportation purposes. The Virginia law mandates that the tax be imposed on the average wholesale price (calculated twice each year) but sets a price floor; if prices of motor fuels fall beneath that floor, the amount of fuel tax charged per gallon is not reduced further.[23]

A federal sales tax on motor fuel would likely be at best an interim solution to the long-term problem of financing transportation infrastructure because, like the current motor fuel tax, it relies on fuel consumption to fund transportation programs. To the extent that improved vehicle efficiency or adoption of hybrid or electric vehicles leads to long-term declines in fuel usage, a sales tax on fuel may not lead to increases in trust fund revenues. In addition, a sales tax calibrated to produce a desired amount of revenue in an environment of high motor fuel prices could significantly underperform if fuel prices were to be lower than anticipated.[24]

Reforms to the Current Fuel-Tax Structure

"Fixing" the Gas Tax

A differently designed gas tax might be indexed to both inflation (either inflation generally or in construction costs) and fuel-efficiency growth. [25] This new design would be imposed after raising the current gas tax rate to compensate for the loss in purchasing power since the last rate increase in 1993.[26] One bill with some of these attributes is the Update, Promote, and Develop America's Transportation Essentials Act (UPDATE; H.R. 3636), introduced by Representative Earl Blumenauer. The bill would raise the tax rates on gasoline, diesel, and kerosene by 15 cents over three years: by eight cents per gallon for 2014; by four cents per gallon for 2015, and by three cents per gallon for 2016. The full 15-cent increase is authorized through the end of 2025. The rates would be adjusted annually for inflation. The bill does not provide for an adjustment for gains in fuel efficiency.

An alternative approach might take advantage of movements in fuel prices to make tax increases seem less burdensome to highway users, perhaps by providing a tax increase to take effect only when the price of gasoline falls below a specified threshold. Another option would increase all highway taxes, not just the fuel taxes, so that the package could be presented as an increase in highway user charges rather than simply a hike in the gasoline tax.[27]

Distance-Based (VMT) Charges

Both study commissions created by SAFETEA recommended charging drivers based on vehicle miles traveled to fund federal surface transportation activities.[28] Fees based on vehicle miles traveled have been discussed in the transportation world for years, and have been the subject of extensive study by the Transportation Research Board (TRB)[29] and other groups. The conclusions reached by these studies almost universally suggest that a transition to a VMT system of financing is desirable and feasible. These same studies, nonetheless, suggest that transition to a VMT system would take time, and they identify numerous obstacles to implementation. The most common recommendation is that the transition process begin on a pilot basis, to gain experience prior to potential national adoption.

Federal VMT charges could be used to provide revenue to the HTF, either in place of or alongside federal motor fuel taxes. Certain classes of vehicles might remain subject to fuel taxes even after a VMT charge is put into place. It is also possible that a VMT charge might be used in addition to other revenue-raising measures.

Distance charges are viewed by economists as being a superior form of user charge. Although the fuel tax is often referred to as a user fee, it is better understood as a proxy for a user fee because fuel use does not directly correspond to the quantity (miles) of infrastructure consumed. A hybrid car and a gasoline-powered sport utility vehicle making the same trip, for example, use the same amount of infrastructure (highway miles), but pay different amounts of tax based on the fuel efficiency of the vehicles. With a VMT charge, by contrast, the amount paid would be directly related to the amount of road miles used. Adding vehicle weight into the equation might result in a charge that more fully incorporates infrastructure use by reflecting the pavement wear attributable to the vehicle as well.[30]

VMT charges have two particular attractions. One is that all road users would have to pay, whereas current drivers of vehicles powered by batteries, fuel cells, or other alternative technologies are able to use public roads without paying the fuel taxes used to improve them. The other is that a VMT charge can be adjusted to reflect the full costs of using a particular segment of infrastructure. For example, it can be set at a higher level on a heavily used urban highway than on a lightly used rural road. It can be varied by time, traffic level, or some other measure to reflect congestion on a road segment as it occurs, giving drivers price signals that might encourage them to change their driving patterns to avoid crowded roads or rush hours, perhaps even precluding the need for new construction or highway improvements.

Distance-related charges have a long history in the transportation sector. A few states impose weight and distance taxes on trucks, and many toll roads base their toll structure on miles traveled and the number of axles on a vehicle, which is used as a proxy for weight. The barrier to implementing distance-based fees on road users has always been finding an efficient means of measuring usage and collecting the corresponding fees.

The technology to assess and collect VMT charges already exists to some extent thanks to the widespread adoption of high-capacity electronics in new vehicles, combined with cellular communications technologies and integrated global positioning systems (GPS). Implementing a VMT system in the United States, however, would require a clear set of technical standards to enable the collection and processing of the information generated by this technology on a uniform basis. There are also privacy, cost, and administrative hurdles that would need to be addressed.

Privacy Issues

The same technology that makes VMT charges possible is probably the major barrier to implementation. As a Florida newspaper editorialized,

> It's not the government's business to know about everyone's whereabouts. A VMT pilot program in South Florida will use a tracking device to log drivers' mileage. Impose the VMT, and Big Brother, for all intents and purposes, will be in the back seat. Tracking your comings and goings isn't akin to installing cameras at intersections to catch red-light-runners who threaten anyone's safety, an effective measure we heartily endorse that saves lives. It's a gratuitous intrusion into drivers' lives. And an intrusion that policymakers need to steer clear of.[31]

Research suggests that it is the GPS tracking involved in some proposed collection schemes that causes the most unease.[32] Alternative technologies would allow tracking of vehicle mileage without the use of GPS. A well-known pilot study in Oregon relied on a periodic odometer reading of each vehicle, which could be done at some fixed interval by visiting a special facility, or else during refueling at a gas station equipped to record an electronically transmitted odometer reading. Another approach would use cellular-linked technology, such as a weekly automated contact between a vehicle and a collection center, to collect mileage information without disclosing details about individual travel. These less sophisticated reporting systems, however, would not be well suited to implementing variable pricing mechanisms.

Depending on the collection technology required for a VMT system, drivers of older vehicles could face the need to install potentially costly equipment. A VMT system could avoid this problem by allowing owners of older vehicles to continue to pay fuel taxes until they replace their vehicles. This, however, would increase the complexity and administrative cost of the system.

Pricing

In principle, a VMT system could be revenue neutral; that is, the rate charged per mile could be set to equal the fuel tax paid by an average driver in the course of driving one mile. According to some studies, this would probably mean a fee of around 1 cent per mile initially.[33]

Individual drivers, however, do not necessarily pay "average" fuel taxes. While a VMT charge of around 1 cent per mile may be revenue neutral across the universe of American drivers, it may be more or less costly than the current motor fuel taxes for an individual driver. Some vehicle owners, such as those who have paid a premium to buy a hybrid vehicle that uses little fuel, may face higher costs with a VMT system—and may object to paying the same charges as an individual driving a fuel-inefficient SUV.

Such concerns introduce issues of social equity into the VMT rate-setting process. In theory, economists generally agree that drivers should pay the full "social cost" of their vehicles, but there is little agreement about what those costs are. Attempting to reward certain classes of vehicles with lower charges might raise further barriers to public acceptance of VMT charges. Conversely, the case may be made that charging VMTs to hybrid and all electric vehicles' use might discourage their purchase.

Setting initial charges at the revenue-neutral level would pose a further problem. One argument for moving to VMT charges is that fuel taxes are providing insufficient funds for transportation infrastructure. If a VMT charge is to provide additional revenue, then by definition it cannot be revenue neutral, and would initially need to be higher than 1 cent per mile. Nor would raising a VMT rate on a periodic basis be easier politically than raising the fuel taxes has been. One solution for this problem would be to index a VMT charge to some inflation measure, but this would likely have the same political issues as indexation of the existing fuel taxes, an idea that has not been enacted by Congress.

Transition Costs/Complexity

A major advantage of the federal fuel tax system is its low cost of collection. Less than 1% of revenue is devoted to collection. In part this is due to the relatively small number of places where the fuel tax is collected: it is paid not at the fuel pump, but at the so-called "first point of distribution," normally a refinery or a tank farm.[34] This collection system reduces the opportunity for fraud and theft and also saves money, because it is much easier administratively to collect taxes from a few rather than many locations and firms.[35]

A VMT charge portends a far broader collection system. Depending on the technology employed, the number of collection locations could be extremely large. Experience in Germany, where trucks using the autobahns pay VMT charges, suggests that the cost of collecting a VMT charge could be 6% or more of collections, although that might decline over time.[36] Billing could be a major administrative challenge. Based on 2012 figures, there are roughly 250 million privately owned motor vehicles in the United States.[37] Each of these vehicles is a potential tax collection point.

Obviously the transition from a tax collected at a few places to a fee collected at many places creates efficiency issues. Also relevant in this context are questions about a possible rise in avoidance and fraud, both of which, in the history of fuel tax collection, occurred more frequently when more collection points existed. These complexities would need to be overcome for a VMT charge to become an efficient source of revenue.

VMT and Non-highway Programs

Since 1982, when the transit account within the highway trust fund was established, there has been an unwritten truce between highway and other transportation interests not to reopen the debate over funding non-highway programs from the trust fund. The move to a VMT charge would reopen this debate. If the VMT charge were collected strictly from motorists and applied only to highway financing, it might reasonably be characterized as a user fee, even if, as noted above, the amount paid by each individual driver would not correspond precisely to the social cost of that user's driving. If, instead, the amounts collected by a VMT charge were distributed among various transportation modes, the charge might appear more as a tax, and Congress would face consideration of the future of non-highway programs now financed through the HTF.

Other Options to Preserve the Highway Trust Fund

In addition to options discussed above, a wide range of additional proposals has been suggested to generate revenue for the highway trust fund. These proposals largely originated from the work of the two SAFETEA congressional commissions and of groups such as AASHTO and TRB.[38] An AASHTO table showing estimates of the amounts of revenues from various sources could be produced for surface transportation over a six-year period is reproduced in **Figure 1**.

Matrix of Illustrative Surface Transportation Revenue Options

(all revenue estimates in $ millions)

Funding Mechanisms	Mechanism Yield 2014			Illustrative Rate	Revenues 2014	Average Revenues 2015-2020	Total Revenues 2015-2020
Container Tax	$1.00 per TEU=	$	421	$15.00	$ 6,317	$ 6,898	$ 41,361
Customs Revenues (Partial Dedication)	1.0% of Receipts =	$	357	1.0%	$ 357	$ 408	$ 2,451
Drivers License Surcharge (Annual)	$1.00 Surcharge=	$	222	$5.00	$ 1,108	$ 1,154	$ 6,926
Excise Tax on Diesel (Increase)	1¢ per Gallon =	$	399	15.0¢	$ 5,983	$ 6,480	$ 38,877
Excise Tax on Diesel (Indexing)	n/a				$ 440	$ 1,031	$ 6,183
Excise Tax on Gasoline (Increase)	1¢ per Gallon =	$	1,282	10.0¢	$ 12,823	$ 13,367	$ 80,202
Excise Tax on Gasoline (Indexing)	n/a				$ 1,046	$ 2,384	$ 14,308
Freight Bill - All Modes	1.0% of Sales =	$	8,318	1.0%	$ 8,318	$ 9,236	$ 55,415
Freight Bill - Truck Only	1.0% of Sales =	$	7,221	1.0%	$ 7,221	$ 8,018	$ 48,110
Freight Charge - All Modes (Ton)	1¢ per Ton =	$	180	25.0¢	$ 4,492	$ 4,988	$ 29,929
Freight Charge - All Modes (Ton-Mile)	1¢ per Ton-mile=	$	47,530	0.5¢	$ 23,765	$ 26,389	$ 158,334
Freight Charge - Truck Only (Ton)	1¢ per Ton =	$	124	25.0¢	$ 3,098	$ 3,440	$ 20,641
Freight Charge - Truck Only (Ton-Mile)	1¢ per Ton-mile=	$	13,911	0.5¢	$ 6,956	$ 7,724	$ 46,342
Harbor Maintenance Tax (Increase)	0.1% Tax =	$	1,331	0.5%	$ 6,657	$ 7,264	$ 43,584
Heavy Vehicle Use Tax (Increase)	100% Increase=	$	852	15.0%	$ 128	$ 163	$ 977
Imported Oil Tax	$1.00 per Barrel =	$	3,528	$1.00	$ 3,528	$ 3,528	$ 21,171
Income Tax - Business (Partial Dedication)	0.1% of Current Taxes =	$	440	1.0%	$ 4,396	$ 4,847	$ 29,082
Income Tax - Personal (Partial Dedication)	0.1% of Current Taxes =	$	1,508	1.0%	$ 15,084	$ 18,393	$ 110,356
Oil, Gas, Minerals Lease - Rent, Bonus, and Other Income (Partial Dedication)	1.0% of GF Revenues =	$	15	50.0%	$ 750	$ 750	$ 4,500
Oil, Gas, Minerals Lease - Royalties (Partial Dedication)	1.0% of GF revenues =	$	55	50.0%	$ 2,750	$ 2,750	$ 16,500
Registration Fee on Light Duty Vehicles (Annual)	$1.00 Fee=	$	259	$10.00	$ 2,594	$ 2,731	$ 16,387
Registration Fee on Trucks (Annual)	$1.00 Fee=	$	9	$15.00	$ 131	$ 133	$ 797
Sales Tax on Auto-related Parts and Services	1.0% of Sales=	$	2,567	1.0%	$ 2,567	$ 2,883	$ 17,299
Sales Tax on Fuel - Diesel	1.0% of Sales =	$	1,253	11.0%	$ 13,782	$ 15,839	$ 95,033
Sales Tax on Fuel - Gasoline	1.0% of Sales =	$	3,711	8.0%	$ 29,686	$ 31,126	$ 186,753
Sales Tax on New and Used Light Duty Vehicles	1.0% of Sales=	$	2,619	1.0%	$ 2,619	$ 2,619	$ 15,715
Sales Tax on New Light Duty Vehicles	1.0% of Sales =	$	1,625	1.0%	$ 1,625	$ 1,625	$ 9,752
Sales Tax on Trucks and Trailers (Increase)	1.0% of Sales =	$	268	5.0%	$ 1,340	$ 1,677	$ 10,062
Tire Tax on Light Duty Vehicles	$1.00 Fee=	$	195	$3.00	$ 584	$ 615	$ 3,687
Tire Tax on Trucks (Increase)	100% Increase=	$	434	10.0%	$ 43	$ 54	$ 326
Vehicle Miles Traveled Fee on Light Duty Vehicles (All Miles)	1¢ per VMT =	$	26,891	2.0¢	$ 53,781	$ 55,852	$ 335,111

Source: Provided by AASHTO, Version 11: July 10, 2013.

Figure 1. AASHTO Matrix of Revenue Options with Estimates.

Among the many proposals that have been advanced are freight-related taxes or fees such as a freight waybill tax, container fee, or terminal facility charge; the dedication of some portion of customs duties or fees for leases for drilling on federal lands or ocean areas, which are deposited in the general fund, to freight-related port-of-entry infrastructure; a broad-based carbon tax; and many smaller fees and surcharges. It should be emphasized that the revenue estimates above are suggestive rather than precise forecasts. Also, there are variables attached to each estimate that are not delineated. For example, the number of annual auto registrations could turn out to be higher or lower than AASHTO assumed for purposes of revenue estimation.

The Future of the Trust Fund

If Congress chooses not to impose new taxes and fees dedicated to the highway trust fund, it could still maintain or expand the surface transportation program with general fund monies. Any of the financing options discussed above could be used to sustain the existing federal financing mechanism, the highway trust fund, but could also be used to support the general fund if Congress wishes to consider alternatives to the trust fund financing model. This would be a significant departure from past practice, and would weaken the historical link between the taxes and fees paid by highway users and spending on the nation's highways and bridges.

The trust fund was set up as a temporary device that was supposed to disappear when the Interstate system was finished. It has endured, and its breadth of financing has expanded well beyond the Interstates. But it is certainly not essential to a federal role in transportation finance. Congress routinely funds large infrastructure projects, such as those constructed by the Army Corps of Engineers, from general fund appropriations. Before 1956, it funded highway and other transportation projects using annual appropriations. As recently as the 1990s, significant highway programs such as the Appalachian Highway System were funded from the general fund.

One alternative would be to devote the trust fund to highway-related programs integral to the national network such as the Interstate Highways, the national highway system, key bridge infrastructure, and the Federal Lands Highway Program. This would leave transit and other surface transportation programs to be funded exclusively by annual appropriations of general funds. On February 9, 2012, such a proposal was reported out of the House Committee on Ways and Means in the American Energy and Infrastructure

Jobs Financing Act of 2012 (H.R. 7, 112th Congress). The bill would have dedicated all highway tax revenue to highways. Transit would have been funded via an alternative transportation account with general fund monies. This change was met by strong opposition and was not included in MAP-21.

Restricting trust fund spending to highways would have political implications. Since the early 1990s, transit and cycling advocates, environmentalists, and a wide range of other groups have become full-fledged supporters of the surface transportation program, as it has benefited their interests. The expanded coalition supporting the surface transportation program played an important role in the hard-fought political battles of the mid-1990s that gave the trust fund accounts special status as separate accounts in the budget. This special status broadened support for large spending increases in each of the last two reauthorization bills that preceded MAP-21. The desire for increased spending included support for keeping unexpended balances in the HTF as low as possible.

The 1998 budget changes, which gave the highway account and the transit account special status within the budget similar to that enjoyed by the Social Security trust fund, occurred over objections by the appropriations and budget committees, which had previously exerted more control over transportation spending than they do today. MAP-21 did not continue these special status provisions, and appropriators have regained much of the influence they had previously. Eliminating the HTF would reduce the influence of the authorizing committees further and increase the influence of the appropriations committees over surface transportation.

Another alternative would be to eliminate the trust fund structure, thereby doing away with its complicated budget framework of contract authority, obligations, and apportionments.[39] Eliminating the trust fund would force surface transportation to compete with other federal programs for funding each year, possibly leading to less spending on transportation. The general fund transfers to the HTF since FY2008 and the additional infrastructure funding provided by the American Recovery and Reinvestment Act of 2009 (ARRA; P.L. 111-5), however, suggest that Congress is willing to spend money on surface transportation regardless of the revenue source.

There could be advantages to moving away from trust fund financing of surface transportation. Prior to the injection of general fund revenues into the HTF, one of the most intractable arguments in reauthorization debates concerned which states were "donors" to transportation programs and which were "donees." Donor states are states whose highway users are estimated to pay more to the Highway account of the HTF than they receive. Donee states receive more than they pay. The donor-donee dispute was unique to the federal highway program, and occurred largely because of the ability to track federal fuel tax revenues by state. This issue would likely disappear if transportation-related taxes were deposited into the general fund instead of the trust fund. Treating fuel taxes as just another source of federal revenue would also dampen the longstanding link between road user charges and program spending. This would provide Congress with greater flexibility to allocate funding among various transportation modes and between transportation and nontransportation uses.

Eliminating the trust fund might also focus more attention on the costs and benefits of individual surface transportation programs. Most trust-fund outlays take the form of formula grants over which states have a great deal of spending discretion. Especially within the highway program, money can be transferred among programs relatively easily. While there are numerous federal requirements attached to trust fund expenditures, there have been until recently relatively few performance-oriented goals that the states are required to meet in selecting projects to be undertaken with federal monies. MAP-21 included a requirement for the use of performance management throughout the planning process, and this might be easier to implement without formula programs that automatically apportion funding to the states.

Eliminating the trust fund might also allow for creativity in thinking about the provision of transportation infrastructure across the modal boundaries that now define much of federal transportation spending. Historically, important parts of the U.S. transportation infrastructure, such as the transcontinental railroads and the Panama Canal, were authorized by specific congressional enactments rather than grant programs. Reconsidering the trust fund structure might give Congress and the President the opportunity to come up with a new way to fund infrastructure needs.

Toll Financing of Federal-Aid System Highways

During much of the history of federal aid to highways, toll financing was prohibited, discouraged, or relegated to a minor role.[40] Given this, the small share (4.83% in 2011)[41] of overall highway finance provided by tolling is not surprising. The Federal-Aid Highway and Federal Highway Revenue Acts of 1956 (70 Stat. 374; P.L. 84-627), which provided for the construction and financing of the Interstate Highway system, reaffirmed the prohibition of tolling of federal-aid highways. Thirty-five years later, however, the

Intermodal Surface Transportation Efficiency Act of 1991 (ISTEA; P.L. 102-240) opened non-Interstate system highways to tolling, subject to certain limitations (including requiring public jurisdiction over privately owned toll facilities). Both the 1998 Transportation Equity Act for the 21st Century (TEA-21; P.L. 105-178, as amended by P.L. 105-206) and SAFETEA included provisions allowing tolling of some high-occupancy vehicle (HOV) lanes, establishing pilot projects for tolling Interstate system routes, and permitting the use of congestion pricing in some instances.

MAP-21 allows for the tolling of new roads, including new Interstate Highway system roads and extensions. It allows for the reconstruction of existing roads and addition of new capacity lanes (on both Interstate Highways and non-Interstate roads) and their conversion to toll facilities, as long as the total number of "free" lanes is not reduced.[42] The act eliminated the long-standing requirement that a toll agreement be executed with the FHWA prior to tolling a facility under the mainstream (Section 129) tolling program. Despite these changes, MAP-21 retains most of the prior restrictions on the use of toll revenues. MAP-21's changes fit well with support in Congress and in the Obama Administration for the expanded use of congestion pricing.

Significant growth of nationwide toll revenues would require the building of more tolled facilities, conversion of free roads and bridges to toll roads, increases in toll rates on existing toll facilities, or increases in traffic. Augmenting toll road mileage is difficult to accomplish: FHWA statistics identify 5,745 tolled miles of roads, bridges, and tunnels in 2013,[43] a net increase of 1,024 toll road miles, or 22%, over 1990.[44] The changes in the authorization bills since ISTEA do not appear to have led to an increase in toll receipts as a share of total revenues used for highways. Although toll revenues used for highways grew in nominal terms, from $7.75 billion in FY2005 to $9.81 billion in FY2011, they continued to account for approximately 5% of total funds available for highways from all units of government during these years. This is similar to the annual average since FY1955.[45]

Expanded ability of state and local governments to impose tolls on federal-aid highways could make it easier for them to build projects that might otherwise be delayed. Another advantage of tolls is that they can provide the cash flow necessary to attract private financing of road projects or to support public-private partnerships (P3s) and other innovative financing techniques (such as those discussed later in this report). Unlike VMT charges, tolls are broadly familiar to the driving public. (Currently, 35 states have at least one toll road, bridge, or tunnel.) Variable tolls designed to keep traffic in the toll facility flowing freely are already in use on a number of roads, including lanes recently constructed on the Washington Capital Beltway (I-495) in Virginia.

Table 2 briefly describes the provisions of *U.S. Code* Title 23 that now govern the tolling of federal-aid highways.

Table 2. Active Federal Tolling Programs

Program	Intent
Section 129 Exceptions to the Freedom from Tolls Provision	Authorizes up to 80% federal participation in the initial construction of a toll road, bridge, tunnel, or ferry (both interstate system and non-interstate roads); reconstruction of existing toll facilities; reconstruction of a toll-free federal-aid highway (Interstate or non-Interstate) and conversion to a toll facility so long as the facility has the same number of toll-free lanes after construction as it did before; and preliminary studies to determine toll facility feasibility. Facility must be publicly owned or, if privately owned, under contract to a public authority.
High Occupancy Vehicle (HOV) Facilities	Section 166 of Title 23 allows states to charge tolls on vehicles that do not meet the occupancy requirements for HOV lane use (including HOVs on the Interstate system).
Interstate System Reconstruction and Rehabilitation Toll Pilot Program	Allows tolls on three pilot projects in different states to reconstruct an existing Interstate system highway and convert it to a tolled facility. Originally passed in 1998.
Value Pricing Pilot Program	Provides funds for local transportation programs to try the value pricing approaches to managing congestion, including use of tolling. No dedicated funding under MAP-21.

Source: FHWA. Title 23 U.S.C. §§129, 166, 301. P.L. 112-141.

Options for Expanded Use of Tolling

Congress has numerous options if it opts to expand the role of tolling in surface transportation finance. Among them are the following:

- It might require that most or all new construction on the federal-aid system be toll-financed. This would relieve the demands on the HTF or the general fund as sources of revenue for new highway construction.[46]
- It could consider making all Interstate system highways eligible for conversion to toll roads. The Interstates carry high traffic volumes relative to other roads and likely make up much of the road mileage that could generate sufficient toll revenues to support toll finance. In urban areas, increased tolling could have the added benefit of reducing congestion. Allowing tolls on existing Interstates would overturn the "freedom from tolls" provision of the Federal-Aid Highway Act of 1956.[47]
- An even broader alternative would be to allow states to toll any federal-aid highway. Such authorizations might, or might not, encourage further use of tolls that vary by time of day or by degree of congestion.
- Legislation could further encourage private entities to pursue toll road projects on the federal-aid highway system, presumably by constructing additional lanes or interchanges.

One issue in the expansion of tolling is the extent to which state and local governments could use increased toll revenues to substitute for other spending, reducing the net impact of a more expansive federal tolling policy. If the aim of a policy of expanded use of tolling is to increase total spending on transportation infrastructure, it would be necessary to ensure that state and local governments not simply use revenues from tolls on federal-aid highways to replace current transportation outlays. Another issue is one of timing. Even a broad policy shift toward tolling, such as converting the Interstate highway system to tolling as it is reconstructed, would take many years and would provide little relief in the near term.

Obstacles to the Expanded Use of Tolling

Greater reliance on tolls as a source of federal highway funding faces significant obstacles, not least the general public hostility to tolls. Title 23 (Highways) of the *U.S. Code* imposes certain limitations on the use of toll revenues, but FHWA exercises no authority over toll rates, either on roads or on bridges, and thus has little direct influence over the amount of money raised.

Some states already rely on tolls as an important source of income. Florida, New Jersey, New York, Pennsylvania, and Illinois receive over 10% of their annual highway revenues from tolls.[48] On the other hand, there are 15 states and the District of Columbia that have no toll facilities.[49]

At the local level, expanded use of tolling faces a number of challenges beyond general public hostility.[50] Revenue projections from planned toll facilities generally do not cover project costs, and some states find it hard to garner public support for toll projects that also require public subsidization. For toll projects with private partners, often either a public subsidy is needed or competing free facilities must be converted to toll facilities for the projects to make business sense. In some cases, proposed toll projects have raised public concerns about diversion of traffic, especially trucks, from the tolled roads to adjacent free roads. In addition, revenues do not always meet projections, potentially leaving financial burdens on local governments.[51]

Trucking interests generally oppose tolling.[52] Major trucking companies have expressed a preference for raising fuel taxes but requiring that the increased revenues go exclusively for highway improvement. Independent truckers generally prefer the status quo, but also view federal fuel tax increases as preferable to tolls.[53] One reason for the preference for fuel taxes is that studies have concluded that funding highways with motor fuel taxes provide trucks a cross-subsidy from automobile users' gas tax payments.[54] Also, since toll rates are controlled locally, trucking interests are concerned that local officials may find it an attractive option to set high rates on trucks, whose shipments are often not local, and low rates on cars.

Views on the Potential of Toll Financing

There have been few systematic estimates of the potential for tolls to generate revenues for highway construction. A 2006 TRB report, *Future Financing Options to Meet Highway and Transit Needs*, estimated that aggressive use of the tolling and pricing opportunities in SAFETEA had the potential to generate an average additional $1.1 billion in revenue per year during 2010 to 2017, reaching an additional $2.4 billion in 2017.[55] Another TRB publication from 2006, *The Fuel Tax and Alternatives for Transportation Funding*, argued that an aggressive program of "toll conversion and new toll road development following the models of the HOT networks and FAST lanes proposals might raise additional revenue equal to the tolls already being collected on U.S. highways (that is about $10 billion per year or less)."[56]

Some more recent commentaries, however, have expressed caution in projecting revenues from high-occupancy toll (HOT) lanes and other tolled express lanes, warning that "HOT lanes are not necessarily big generators of revenue ... most projects—particularly HOV-to-HOT expansion projects—barely cover ongoing expenses for management and operations, much less offset the capital costs."[57] Another article examining the value pricing experience of I-15 in San Diego found that it generated only enough revenue to cover operating costs, pay for the California Highway Patrol to enforce vehicle occupancy rules, and provide a small amount to support bus services on I-15.[58] In 2008, AASHTO president Pete Rahn testified before the House Transportation and Infrastructure Committee that "[e]ven the most optimistic forecasts project that this revenue source [tolls] would only meet seven to nine percent of investment needs nationally in the future."[59]

Using tolling to reduce the need for HTF resources and to avoid revenue increases or program reductions would require a major expansion of tolling. Examples of three scenarios that could do this include the following. First, there could be further expansion of leveraging programs[60] to finance new roads and bridges. This could lead to an increase in toll roads because leveraging programs generally require a revenue stream to support the debt that the program incurs, and tolls are a common choice of repayment mechanism. For example, the Transportation Infrastructure Finance and Innovation Act (TIFIA) program, discussed later in this report, might be again expanded. Appropriations, however, would be needed to cover the federal subsidy costs of such programs. Second, Congress might direct that all Interstate system highways be converted to toll roads over time as the system is expanded or reconstructed. This change alone would eventually shift roughly a fourth of the nation's vehicle miles traveled to a toll-based system. However, assuming users would continue to pay fuel taxes, the issue of double taxation could arise unless fuel taxes used on the Interstate Highways are rebated.[61] This policy might be difficult to develop by September 2014, when MAP-21 expires, or to implement broadly within the time frame of the next reauthorization bill. It could be considered as part of a longer-term solution to funding needs. Finally, the weight and distance charges commonly used in tolling are very similar to those of a VMT charge. Therefore, a VMT charge could be considered a toll by another name.

VALUE CAPTURE

Value capture represents an attempt to cover part or all of the cost of transportation improvements from landowners or developers who benefit from the resulting increase in the value of real property. Value capture revenue mechanisms include tax increment financing, special assessments, development impact fees, negotiated exactions, and joint development.[62] The federal role in value capture strategies may be limited, as the Government Accountability Office (GAO) has noted,[63] but it is worth describing these strategies to provide a fuller picture of the ways in which they might supplement or supplant more commonly used funding and financing mechanisms.

Value capture is not a new idea. Land developers built and operated streetcar systems in the late 19th century as a way to sell houses on the urban fringe, for example. Much of the recent experience with value capture has been associated with public transit. GAO found that the most widely used mechanism is joint development, in which a real estate project at or near a transit station is pursued cooperatively between the public and private sectors. An example might involve a transit agency leasing air rights over a station to a developer in exchange for a regular payment.

GAO found that joint development has generated relatively small amounts of money for transit agencies.[64] For example, the Metropolitan Atlanta Rapid Transit Authority expected about $4 million from such deals in FY2008, about 1% of its $374 million operating budget. However, less widely used strategies, such as special assessment districts, are estimated to generate significant amounts of funding for specific projects. A special assessment district in Seattle produced $25 million of the $53 million (47%) needed to fund the South Lake Union streetcar project.[65]

There has been less use of value capture in highway projects, but this appears to be changing. Texas, for example, has authorized the creation of transportation reinvestment zones to help fund highway projects.[66] Special assessment districts have been set up in several states, including Florida and Virginia, to fund highway projects. In Virginia a special assessment district was used to help fund the expansion of Route 28 near Washington Dulles International Airport beginning in the late 1980s.[67]

PRIVATE FINANCING VIA P3S

Growing demands on the transportation system and constraints on public resources have led to calls for more private-sector involvement in the provision of highway and transit infrastructure through P3s, which can be designed to lessen demands on public-sector funding. Private involvement can take a variety of forms, including design-build and design-build-finance-operate agreements. Typically, the "public" in public-private partnerships refers to a state government, local government, or transit agency. The federal government, nevertheless, exerts influence over the prevalence and structure of P3s through its transportation programs, funding, and regulatory oversight.[68]

To be viable, P3s involving private financing typically require an anticipated project-related revenue stream from a source such as vehicle tolls, container fees, or, in the case of transit station development, building rents. Private-sector resources may come from an initial payment to lease an existing asset in exchange for future revenue, as with the Indiana Toll Road and Chicago Skyway, or they may arise from a newly developed asset that creates a new revenue stream. Either way, a facility user fee is often the key to unlocking private-sector participation and resources.

In some cases, private-sector financing is backed by "availability payments," regular payments made by government to the private entity based on negotiated quality and performance standards of the facility. For example, major improvements to I-595 near Fort Lauderdale, FL, were made by a private company under a 35-year design-build-finance-operate-maintain contract. The Florida Department of Transportation (FDOT) began making availability payments to the private partner when the facility opened in 2014. Toll rates on the new express lanes are set by FDOT, and revenue collected is retained by the state.[69] The financing includes a federal TIFIA loan (see discussion below) and state funds.

It is widely believed that there are hundreds of billions of dollars of private monies available globally for infrastructure investment, such as surface transportation.[70] To date, however, private investment in U.S. highways and transit has been modest in comparison to spending by all levels of government. According to one study, from 1989 through early 2011 there were 96 transportation P3s worth a total of $54.3 billion in the United States; 11 of these projects, totaling $12.4 billion, included a private financing component.[71]

It is quite possible that private investment will grow in the future. In this regard, the seven-fold increase in TIFIA program resources is likely to make some difference. But many impediments remain. Some of the major ones include the relative attractiveness of the tax-exempt financing available to state and local government, political opposition to tolling and privatization, and difficulties associated with project development.[72] Tolling, both public and private, accounts for about 5% of highway revenues. Thus even with aggressive increases in tolling, it may be unrealistic to expect P3s to generate more than 7% to 9% of the future needs of highway and transit infrastructure nationally. Private-sector financing generated through P3s might best be seen as a supplement to traditional public-sector funding rather than as a substitute.

In addition to attracting private capital, P3s may generate new resources for highway and transit infrastructure in at least two ways. First, P3s may improve efficiency through better management and innovation in construction, maintenance, and operation, in effect providing more infrastructure for the same price. Private companies may be more able to examine the full life-cycle cost of investments, whereas public agency decisions are often tied to short-term budget cycles. In the case of the Hudson-Bergen Light Rail in New Jersey, procured under a designbuild-operate-maintain contract, the U.S. Department of Transportation (DOT) estimates saving of 30%, or about $345 million, over the more traditional design-bid-build procurement method.[73] Such cost reductions may not materialize, however, if the public sector has to spend a substantial amount of time on procurement, oversight, dispute resolution, and litigation. For example, the California Department of Transportation has had a number of costly disputes with its private partners.[74] GAO argues that most state governments lack the capacity to manage P3 contracts.[75]

Second, P3s may reduce government agencies' costs by transferring the financial risks of building, maintaining, and operating infrastructure to private investors. These risks include construction delays, unexpectedly high maintenance costs, and the possibility that demand will be less than forecast. There is a danger, however, this transfer of risk may prove illusory if major miscalculations force the public agency to renegotiate contracts or provide financial guarantees.[76] Moreover, as GAO points out, not all the risks can or should be shifted to the private sector. For instance, private investors are unlikely to accept the risk of higher construction costs due to delays in the environmental review process.[77]

TIFIA Financing

An existing federal mechanism for providing credit assistance to relatively large transportation infrastructure projects is financing under TIFIA, enacted in 1998 as part of TEA-21.[78] TIFIA provides federal credit assistance in the form of secured loans, loan guarantees, and lines of credit.

Federal credit assistance provides funds at a relatively low rate and lowers project risk, thereby helping to secure other financing at rates lower than would otherwise be possible. Another purpose of TIFIA funding is to leverage non-federal funding, including investment from the private sector. Loans must be repaid with a dedicated revenue stream, typically a project-related user fee but sometimes also including dedicated tax revenue. As of March 5, 2014, according to FHWA, TIFIA since enactment in 1998 had provided assistance of $15.8 billion to 41 projects. The overall cost of the projects supported is estimated to be $59.9 billion.[79]

MAP-21 greatly enlarged TIFIA by increasing its funding from $122 million annually to $750 million in FY2013 and $1 billion in FY2014. DOT estimates that after administrative costs and application of the obligation limitation it will have $690 million for credit subsidy support in FY2013 and $920 million in FY2014.[80] Assuming an average subsidy cost of 10%, this may provide DOT with the capacity to lend $6.9 billion in FY2013 and $9.2 billion in FY2014.[81] A major reason for the large increase in TIFIA program funding was the great demand for financing, and this has continued. Before the end of FY2013, DOT had received enough applications to exhaust the budget authority made available for FY2013 and FY2014.[82]

Another change made by MAP-21 permits TIFIA credit assistance to be provided for a program of projects secured by a common security pledge. This would be accomplished through a "master credit agreement." Prior to MAP-21, TIFIA only allowed agreements on a project-by-project basis. The Los Angeles County Metropolitan Transportation Authority (Metro), for one, sought this change to accelerate the financing of 12 transit projects (known as the 30/10 Initiative).[83] The master credit agreement also establishes a way to make a commitment of future credit assistance contingent on the availability of funds.

The threshold project cost to be eligible for TIFIA assistance remains $50 million, or $15 million for intelligent transportation system projects, except that MAP-21 includes a threshold of $25 million for rural infrastructure projects. MAP-21 also sets aside 10% of program funds to assist rural projects. Additionally, whereas loans for urban projects must be charged interest not less than the Treasury rate, rural projects that are assisted by the rural setaside are to be offered loans at half the Treasury rate. Rural projects are defined very expansively to include any project in an area other than a city with 250,000 or more inhabitants. MAP-21 also increased the maximum share of project costs that TIFIA may provide from 33% to 49%. One open question is whether the increase in TIFIA's share of project costs to 49% will reduce the non-federal share of project costs and possibly also "crowd out" private financing.

NATIONAL INFRASTRUCTURE BANK

Congress has considered several proposals to create a national infrastructure bank (I-bank) to help finance infrastructure projects.[84] Three I-bank proposals that have been introduced in the 113th Congress are the National Infrastructure Development Bank Act (H.R. 2553), by Representative DeLauro, the American Infrastructure Investment Fund Act (S. 387), by Senators Rockefeller and Lautenberg, and the Partnership to Build America Act (H.R. 2084), by Representative Delaney.

The Partnership to Build America Act (H.R. 2084) proposes to create the American Infrastructure Fund (AIF) as a wholly owned government corporation. The AIF would be funded with $50 billion using repatriated foreign earnings. The companies repatriating the earnings would receive tax benefits in return for investing a certain share of the repatriated earnings in 50-year bonds paying 1%. Transportation facilities would be only one of a number of infrastructure sectors eligible for help from the AIF. Other sectors would be energy, water, communications, and education. Like many I-bank proposals, the AIF would be authorized to make loans and loan guarantees to eligible projects. In addition, H.R. 2084 also permits the AIF to make equity investments (i.e., an ownership stake) up to a maximum of 20% of project costs.

The American Infrastructure Investment Fund Act (S. 387) proposes to create the American Infrastructure Investment Fund that would be a part of the Department of Transportation. Only transportation projects would be eligible for assistance. Financial assistance to projects would be limited to loans and loan guarantees. The act would authorize an appropriation of $5 billion in FY2013 and FY2014.

The National Infrastructure Development Bank Act (H.R. 2553) proposes to create the National Infrastructure Development Bank (NIDB) as a wholly owned government corporation. The NIDB would be authorized to aid transportation, energy, environmental, and telecommunications infrastructure projects. In addition to providing loans and loan guarantees, the NIDB would be permitted to subsidize the interest on a new type of taxable bond called an American Infrastructure Bond (AIB). AIBs could be issued by eligible infrastructure project sponsors. An amount equivalent to the federal taxes paid by AIB holders would be credited to the NDIB for assisting other eligible infrastructure projects.

One purported advantage of an I-bank over other loan programs, such as TIFIA, is that it would have more independence in its operation, such as in project selection, and have greater expertise at its disposal. Additionally, an I-bank is typically set up to help a much wider range of infrastructure projects than a TIFIA program, such as water, energy, and telecommunications infrastructure. Proponents hope the best projects, at least those that are the most financially viable, would be selected from across these sectors.

In many formulations, capitalization of the I-bank comes from an appropriation, but in others an I-bank is authorized to raise its own capital through bond issuance. By issuing nontax-exempt securities, it could tap pools of private capital that do not invest in tax-exempt bonds, the traditional source of much project finance. Tax-exempt municipal securities are unattractive to some investors, either because individual issues are too small to interest them or because the investors do not benefit from the tax preference. Taxable bonds with long maturities might be attractive to such investors, such as pension funds and foreign citizens.[85] An infrastructure bank also might reduce the federal government's share of project costs with greater reliance on nonfederal capital and user fees.

Most infrastructure bank proposals assume the bank would improve the allocation of public resources by funding projects with the highest economic returns regardless of infrastructure system or type. Selection of the projects with the highest returns, however, might conflict with the traditional desire of Congress to assure funding for various purposes. In the extreme case, many transportation projects might not be funded if the bank were to exhaust its lending authority on water or energy projects offering higher returns.

Limitations of an I-bank include its duplication of existing programs like TIFIA and the Wastewater and Drinking Water State Revolving Funds. An infrastructure bank may not be the lowest-cost means of increasing infrastructure spending. CBO has pointed out that a special entity that issues its own debt would not be able to match the lower interest and issuance costs of the U.S. Treasury.[86] In some formulations, a national infrastructure bank exposes the federal government to the risk of default.[87] Others have argued that a national infrastructure bank would be an unnecessary centralization of authority from the state and local level to the federal level. An alternative would be to enhance the operation of state infrastructure banks.

STATE INFRASTRUCTURE BANKS

Instead of creating a national infrastructure bank or fund, it has been suggested that something be done to enhance state infrastructure banks (SIBs) that already exist in many states. Most of these were created in response to a federal state infrastructure bank (SIB) program originally established in surface transportation law in 1995 (P.L. 104-59). According to a recent survey, 32 states had established federally authorized SIBs in 2012.[88] Several states, among them California, Florida, Georgia, Kansas, Ohio, and Virginia, have SIBs that are unconnected to the federal program.[89] Local governments have also begun to embrace the idea. For example, the city of Chicago has established a nonprofit organization, the Chicago Infrastructure Trust, as a way to attract private investment for public works projects.[90] Another example is Dauphin County, PA, which has established an infrastructure bank to make loans to the 40 municipalities and private project sponsors within its borders. Funds for the loans are derived from a state tax on liquid fuels.[91]

One of the one of the biggest stumbling blocks to federally authorized SIBs has been capitalization. This is because federal grant funds that could be used to capitalize a SIB have typically been committed elsewhere. For this reason, one idea is to provide federal funds to states specifically dedicated to SIBs. For example, during the surface transportation reauthorization debate that led to the enactment of MAP-21, it was proposed that $750 million per year be dedicated to SIBs (H.R. 7, 112th Congress). Another proposal was to authorize SIBs to issue a type of tax credit bond (S. 1436, 112th Congress). Neither proposal was enacted.

End Notes

[1] CRS Report R42762, Surface Transportation Funding and Programs Under MAP-21: Moving Ahead for Progress in the 21st Century Act (P.L. 112-141), coordinated by Robert S. Kirk.

[2] H.Rept. 109-203.

[3] CRS Report R42721, Automobile and Truck Fuel Economy (CAFE) and Greenhouse Gas Standards, by Brent D. Yacobucci, Bill Canis, and Richard K. Lattanzio.

[4] Congressional Budget Office, How Would Proposed Fuel Economy Standards Affect the Highway Trust Fund?, Washington, DC, May 2012, http://cbo.gov/sites/default/files /cbofiles/attachments/05-02-CAFE_brief.pdf.

[5] Sarah Puro, "Statement for the Record: Status of the Highway Trust Fund," Congressional Budget Office, Washington, DC, April 24, 2013, p. 4, http://cbo.gov/sites/default/files /cbofiles/attachments/44093- HighwayTrustFund.pdf.

[6] Despite this, two commissions established in SAFETEA, the National Surface Transportation Policy and Revenue Study Commission and the National Surface Transportation Infrastructure Financing Commission, called for increases in federal fuel taxes as the near-term solution; the latter also urged indexing of fuel taxes for inflation and an eventual shift to a financing system based on vehicle miles traveled. See http://www.transportation fortomorrow.com/final_report/index.htm and http://financecommission.dot.gov/Documents /NSTIF_Commission_Final_Report_Mar09FNL.pdf. MAP-21 did not call for additional studies on this subject.

[7] Joint Committee on Taxation, Estimated General Fund and Trust Fund Effects of the Conference Agreement for the Revenue Provisions Contained in Division D of MAP-21, committee print, 112th Cong., 2nd sess., June 28, 2012, JCX58-12, pp. 1-3.

[8] Congressional Budget Office, Highway Trust Fund Projections: CBO February FY2014 Baseline 2013-2024, February 5, 2014. According to CBO, because requests for reimbursement from the HTF may occur at any time while Treasury transfers to the HTF occur only twice each month and requests for reimbursement from the states can vary from month to month, the Federal Highway Administration (FHWA) deems it prudent to maintain a $4 billion minimum in the highway account to prevent having to delay payments to states due to insufficient funds. The equivalent prudent balance in the mass transit account is at least $1 billion.

[9] Ibid.

[10] "Update, Congressional Budget Office 2014 Baseline for 'Highway Bill' Budget Accounts," Transportation Weekly, February 5, 2014.

[11] Contract authority is a type of budget authority that is available for obligation even without an appropriation (although appropriators must eventually provide liquidating authority to permit the eventual outlays). Contract authority is the type of budget authority used by the HTF.

[12] The limitation on obligations (or ObLim) is used to control annual spending in place of an appropriation. The ObLim sets a limit on the total amount of contract authority that can be obligated in a single fiscal year. For practical purposes the ObLim is analogous to an appropriation. Specified "exempt obligations" are not subject to the obligation limitation. "CBO, the HTF and the Highway Bill," Transportation Weekly, February 7, 2014, p. 9, includes, in tabular form, estimates for bills from two through six years in length.

[13] Office of Management and Budget, Budget of the U.S. Government: Appendix, Washington, DC, 2014, pp. 970, 1016.

[14] CRS Report 98-720, Manual on the Federal Budget Process, by Robert Keith and Allen Schick (pdf), 181.

[15] This discussion tracks the changes in the rate of the gasoline tax. Over time other fuels such as diesel have been taxed at different rates. For instance, the current tax on diesel fuel is six cents higher than the gasoline tax. For a tabular history of the rates of the various federal fuel taxes see Federal Highway Administration, Highway Statistics: Table FE101-A, http://www.fhwa.dot.gov/policyinformation/statistics/2009/fe101a.cfm.

[16] CRS Report RL30304, The Federal Excise Tax on Motor Fuels and the Highway Trust Fund: Current Law and Legislative History, by Sean Lowry.

[17] Federal Highway Administration, Financing Federal-aid Highways; Appendix M, Federal Excise Taxes on Highway Motor Fuel, http://www.fhwa.dot.gov/reports/fifahiwy /ffahappm.htm.

[18] U.S. President (Reagan), "Remarks to Reporters Announcing the Administration's Proposal for a Highway and Bridge Repair program: Nov. 23, 1982," The American Presidency Project; Public Papers.

[19] See Congressional Budget Office, How Would Proposed Fuel Economy Standards Affect the Highway Trust Fund?, Washington, CBO, May 2012, p. 3. A drop in outlays in FY2006 helped bring the HTF briefly into balance in FY2006- FY2007.

[20] In 2013, CBO estimated that if the 18.4-cent excise tax on gasoline and the 24.4-cent tax on diesel fuels had been indexed to the CPI, the "tax on gasoline today would be about 29 cents per gallon and the tax on diesel fuels would be about 39 cents per gallon." CBO, Statement for the Record: Status of the Highway Trust Fund, p. 3.

[21] Energy Information Administration, "Petroleum & Other Liquids: Supply and Disposition," http://www.eia.gov/ dnav/pet/pet_sum_snd_a_epd0_mbbl_a_cur.htm.

[22] Jeffrey Ang-Olson, Martin Wachs, and Brian D. Taylor, Variable-Rate State Gasoline Taxes, Institute of Transportation Studies, University of California, Berkeley, Working Paper, UCB-ITS-WP-99-3, July 1999. See also, M. Madowitz and K. Novan, "Gasoline taxes and revenue volatility: an Application to California," Energy Policy, v. 59, 2013, pp 663-673, http://www.sciencedirect.com/science/article/pii/S0301421513002577.

[23] Virginia, House Bill 2313, 2013 session. Wholesale price is the price at the "rack." The price floor is the wholesale price as of February 20, 2013.

[24] A fuel price floor could be established but its impact would depend on how high the floor is set and whether the floor is indexed to inflation. The outcome could still fail to meet revenue expectations.

[25] There are many inflation indexes that could be used, and which one is most appropriate might become an issue of controversy. The most commonly used index is the U.S. Bureau of Labor Statistics' consumer price index (CPI), which, for example, is used to adjust certain aviation user fees. If the 18.3-cent-per-gallon tax that supports the trust fund had been adjusted according to the CPI since the tax took effect in 1993, it would be roughly 30 cents per gallon today.

[26] Institute on Taxation and Economic Policy, A Federal Gas Tax for the Future, Washington, DC, September 2013, pp. 1-13, http://www.itep.org/pdf/fedgastax0913.pdf.

[27] Other highway taxes include taxes on truck and truck trailer sales, heavy tires, and the heavy vehicle use tax.

[28] Finance Commission. p. 5. http://financecommission.dot.gov/Documents/NSTIF_ Commission_Final_Report_Exec_Summary_Feb09.pdf.

[29] Transportation Research Board, National Cooperative Highway Research Program, Implementable Strategies for Shifting to Direct Usage-Based Charges for Transportation Funding, NCHRP Project 20-24(69). Web-Only Document 143. October 2009. http://onlinepubs.trb.org/onlinepubs/nchrp/nchrp_w143.pdf.

[30] Congressional Budget Office, Alternative Approaches to Funding Highways, March 2011, p. 38, http://cbo.gov/sites/ default/files/cbofiles/ftpdocs/121xx/doc12101/03-23-highway funding.pdf.

[31] "Kick mileage tax to the curb before it gets any further," Sun-Sentinel, Fort Lauderdale, September 18, 2009.

[32] Martin Wachs, "After the Motor Fuel Tax: Reshaping Transportation Financing," Issues in Science and Technology, Summer 2009, pp. 85-89; Paul Sorensen, Liisa Ecola, and Martin Wachs, et al., Implementable Strategies for Shifting to Direct Usage-Based Charges for Transportation Funding, National Cooperative Highway Research Program, Transportation

Research Board, NCHRP Web-Only Document 143, Washington, DC, June 2009, http://onlinepubs.trb.org/onlinepubs/nchrp/nchrp_w143.pdf.

[33] Miller Center of Public Affairs, University of Virginia, Well Within Reach: America's New Transportation Agenda, Conference Report, Charlottesville, VA, October 10, 2010, http://web1.millercenter.org/conferences/report/ conf_2009_transportation.pdf.

[34] This is often referred to as collecting at the "rack." According to the Internal Revenue Service, in 2013 there were 850 registered taxpayers at the "rack."

[35] This 1% cost of collection figure has recently been challenged; see Daryl S. Fleming, Dispelling the Myths: Toll and Fuel Tax Collection Costs in the 21st Century, Reason Foundation, Culver City, CA, November 2012, http://reason.org/ files/dispelling_toll_and_gas_tax_collection_myths.pdf.

[36] Estimates of the administrative costs that could be associated with a national VMT fee collection system vary dramatically. In part this is due to the lack of experience with VMT charge collection. A tax imposed on trucks using the German autobahn system is perhaps the closest example of a currently operating system VMT system. In scale and scope, however, it is much different from the national system under discussion in this CRS report: http://utcm.tamu.edu/mbuf/2010/proceedings/US-deployment-panel.stm.

[37] Federal Highway Administration, 2012 Highway Statistics, http://www.fhwa.dot.gov/policy information/statistics/ 2012/mv1.cfm.

[38] The Transportation Research Board, through its research programs, has prepared several reports on future surface transportation finance that discuss VMT and other options, including National Cooperative Highway Research Program (NCHRP), "Future Financing Options to Meet Highway and Transit Needs," NCHRP Project 20-24, Web-Only Document 102, December 2006, available at http://onlinepubs.trb.org/onlinepubs /nchrp/nchrp_w102.pdf; and Transportation Research Board, The Fuel Tax and Alternatives for Transportation Funding, Special Report 285, January 2006, available at http://onlinepubs.trb.org/onlinepubs/sr/sr285.pdf.

[39] Joshua Schank and Nikki Rudnick-Thorpe, End of the Highway Trust Fund? Long-Term Options for Funding Federal Surface Transportation, Bipartisan Policy Center, Washington, DC, November 10, 2010, http://amonline.trb.org/12l3f1/12l3f1/1.

[40] The post-World War II toll road construction, most of which was "grandfathered" into the Interstate system, was done on the initiative of the states. Prior to the passage of the 1956 act, the states were far more active in road construction and spending on roads, spending nearly six times what the federal government did in 1955.

[41] Federal Highway Administration, Highway Statistics 2011: Funding for Highways and Disposition of Highway-User Revenues, All Units of Government, 2011, Table HF-10, Washington, DC, March 2013, http://www.fhwa.dot.gov/ policyinformation/statistics/2011 /hf10.cfm.

[42] This loosens the restrictions on the tolling of Interstate Highways, but tightens them on the non-Interstate roads.

[43] Federal Highway Administration, Toll Facilities of the United States: Toll Mileage Trends 2003-2013, "FHWA-PL11-032," July 2013, http://www.fhwa.dot.gov/policyinformation /tollpage/miletrends.cfm. The 5,745 miles of toll roads, bridges, and tunnels compare with the total federal-aid highway eligible road length of 1,001,874 miles (0.57%).

[44] Federal Highway Administration, Toll Facilities in the United States: Bridges-Roads-Tunnels-Ferries, "Publication No: FHWA-PL-91-009," 1991, p. v.

[45] Federal Highway Administration, Highway Statistics: Summary to 1975, Table HF-211, 1977, pp. 107-136. Also Highway Statistics: Summary to 1995, Table SF-210 and Highway

Statistics, various years, Tables SF-21, HF-10 and HF-10a. Also "Figure 6-6: Toll Facility Revenue: 1993-2008," Our Nation's Highways: 2010, http://www.fhwa.dot.gov/policy information/pubs/pl10023/fig6_6.cfm. Toll revenues grew during FY1993-FY2008 at an average annual rate approaching 8%.

[46] According to FHWA, 60% to 70% of toll project revenues are used to pay for new highway, bridge, and tunnel capacity, compared with 20% of total highway revenues. See Current Toll Road Activity in the U.S.: a Survey and Analysis, by Benjamin Perez and Steve Lockwood, Federal Highway Administration, January 2009, p. 21.

[47] See CRS Report R42402, Tolling of Interstate Highways: Issues in Brief, by Robert S. Kirk.

[48] Benjamin Perez and Steve Lockwood, Current Toll Road Activity in the U.S.: A Survey and Analysis, Federal Highway Administration, January 2009, pp. 2-3, http://www.fhwa.dot.gov /ipd/pdfs/ 2008_toll_activity_white_paper.pdf.

[49] Federal Highway Administration, Toll Facilities of the United States: Table T-1, September 2013, http://www.fhwa.dot.gov/policyinformation/tollpage/cover.cfm. The data in Table T-1 are based on voluntary responses received biennially.

[50] U.S. Government Accountability Office, Highway Finance: States' Expanding Use of Tolling Illustrates Diverse Challenges and Strategies, GAO-06-554, June 2006, pp. 32-42, http://www.gao.gov/new.items/d06554.pdf. See also GAO, Highways and Transit: Private Sector Sponsorship of and Investment in Major Projects Has Been Limited, GAO-04-419, March 2004, pp. 20-24, http://www.gao.gov/new.items/d04419.pdf.

[51] Dan Weikel, "State probes fiscal health of O.C. Toll Roads," Los Angeles Times, December 12, 2012.

[52] American Trucking Association, Issue: Tolls on the Interstate System, http://www.trucking.org /AdvIssues/HighwayInf_Fund/Tolls/Issue%20Paper%20-%20Tolls%20on%20the%20 Interstate%20System.pdf. See also: "Trucking Industry Still Prefers Gas Tax over Tolling for Highway Repair Funding," Daily Report for Executives, September 8, 2006.

[53] Owner-Operator Independent Drivers Association, http://www.ooida.com/.

[54] For the relative costs to the road network of use by different classes of vehicles, see http://www.fhwa.dot.gov/policy/ hcas/summary/sum2.html.

[55] Alan E. Pisarski and Martin Wachs, Future Financing Options to Meet Highway and Transit Needs, National Cooperative Highway Research Program, Transportation Research Board, NCHRP Web-Only Document 102, December 2006, pp. ES-8, F-9, http://onlinepubs.trb.org /onlinepubs/nchrp/nchrp_w102.pdf. The National Surface Transportation Policy and Revenue Study Commission, Final Report, used the NCHRP estimates.

[56] Transportation Research Board, Fuel Tax and Alternatives for Transportation Funding, Special Report 285, 2006, p. 154, http://onlinepubs.trb.org/onlinepubs/sr/sr285.pdf. "Fast Lanes" are electronically tolled express lanes with tolls set to limit traffic to the free-flowing maximum; the regular adjoining lanes would be free. The Express Lanes Demonstration Program enacted in SAFETEA is a version of the Fast Lanes proposal.

[57] Ginger Goodin and Chuck Fuhs, "Tolled Managed Lanes: Lessons Learned and Challenges to Meet," TR News, no. 263 (July-August 2009), pp. 20-21.

[58] Derek Toups, "What's in Store for Second-Generation Express Lanes in San Diego?," TR News, no. 263 (July-August 2009), p. 24.

[59] U.S. Congress, House Committee on Transportation and Infrastructure, Hearing on State Perspectives on Transportation for Tomorrow, Recommendations of the National Surface Transportation Policy and Revenue Study Commission, Testimony by Pete Rahn, 110th Cong., 2nd sess., February 13, 2008.

[60] Leveraging programs all involve debt financing.

[61] Robert W. Poole, Jr., Interstate 2.0: Modernizing the Interstate Highway System via Toll Finance, Reason Foundation, Policy Study 423, September 2013, p. 44 p.

[62] Adeel Lari, David Levinson, and Zhirong Zhao, et al., Value Capture for Transportation Finance: Technical Research Report, Center for Transportation Studies, University of Minnesota, June 2009, http://www.cts.umn.edu/ Research/Featured/ValueCapture /index.html.

[63] Government Accountability Office, Public Transportation: Federal Role in Value Capture Strategies for Transit Is Limited, but Additional Guidance Could Help Clarify Policies, GAO-10-781, July 2010, http://www.gao.gov/ new.items/d10781.pdf.

[64] Ibid., p. 16.

[65] Ibid., p. 20.

[66] Sharada Vadali, Rafael Manuel-Aldrete, and Arturo Bujanda, et al., Transportation Reinvestment Zone Handbook, Texas Transportation Institute, College Station, TX, 2011, http://ntl.bts.gov/lib/37000/37800/37821/0-6538- P1_Handbook_resub_editjd_sv.pdf.

[67] For more information, see http://www.28freeway.com/index.html.

[68] CRS Report R43410, Highway and Public Transportation Infrastructure Provision Using Public-Private Partnerships (P3s), by William J. Mallett.

[69] Florida Department of Transportation, I-595 Improvements, District 4, Project Overview, November 1, 2012, http://www.i-595.com/documents/PressRoom/Newsletters/Archived-Overviews/2012-11-01_I595_Project_Summary.pdf.

[70] U.S. Department of Transportation, "Over $400 Billion Available Today for Road, Bridge and Transit Projects U.S. Secretary of Transportation Mary E. Peters Announces," Press Release, DOT 43-08, Wednesday, March 26, 2008; Ken Orski, "A $400 Billion Solution," Innovation Briefs, Vol. 19, No. 8, March 10, 2008.

[71] William Reinhardt, The Role of Private Investment in Meeting U.S. Transportation Infrastructure Needs, The American Road & Transportation Builders Association Transportation Development Foundation, May 2011, http://www.artba.org/mediafiles /transportationp3whitepaper.pdf.

[72] Ibid., pp. 33-37.

[73] U.S. Department of Transportation, Report to Congress on Public-Private Partnerships (Washington, DC, 2004), pp. 38-39, http://www.fhwa.dot.gov/reports/pppdec2004 /pppdec2004.pdf.

[74] Testimony of Alan Lowenthal, Chair, California Senate Transportation and Housing Committee, U.S. Congress, House Committee on Transportation and Infrastructure, Subcommittee on Highways and Transit, Hearing on Public-Private Partnerships: State and User Perspectives, 110th Congress, 1st sess., May 24, 2007.

[75] Government Accountability Office, Federal-Aid Highways: Increased Reliance on Contractors Can Pose Oversight Challenges for Federal and State Officials, GAO-08-198, 2008, http://www.gao.gov/new.items/d08198.pdf.

[76] Engel, E., R. Fischer, and A. Galetovic, "Privatizing Highways in the United States," Review of Industrial Organization, Vol. 29, 2006, pp. 27-53.

[77] Government Accountability Office, Highway Public-Private Partnerships, February 2008.

[78] 23 U.S.C. §601 et seq.

[79] U.S. Department of Transportation, Federal Highway Administration, "TIFIA Approved Projects," http://www.fhwa.dot.gov/ipd/tifia/projects_project_profiles/index.htm.

[80] Department of Transportation, "Letters of Interest for Credit Assistance Under the Transportation Infrastructure Finance and Innovation Act (TIFIA) Program," 77 Federal

Register 45411-45415, July 31, 2012, http://www.fhwa.dot.gov/ipd/pdfs/tifia/fy2013_tifia_nofa_073112.pdf.

81 The subsidy cost is "the estimated long-term cost to the government of a direct loan or a loan guarantee, calculated on a net present value basis, excluding administrative costs," Federal Credit Reform Act of 1990 (FCRA), §502 (5A).

82 In FY2013, as of July 24, 2013, DOT had received requests for a total of $15.8 billion in loans to help finance 31 projects. Total loan capacity over the two years covered by MAP-21 is about $16 billion. Testimony of Anthony Foxx, Secretary of Transportation, U.S. Congress, Senate Environment and Public Works, Oversight Hearing on Implementation of MAP-21's TIFIA Program Enhancements, 113th Cong., 1st sess., July 24, 2013, http://www.epw.senate.gov/public/index.cfm?FuseAction=Files.View&FileStore_id=9a3ecfde-0783-4744-ace6- d825ff352fe.

83 Los Angeles County Metropolitan Transportation Authority (Metro), Metro's 30/10 Initiative, http://libraryarchives.metro.net/DB_Attachments/100524_30_10_Initiative.pdf.

84 For legislation introduced through the 112th Congress, see CRS Report R42115, National Infrastructure Bank: Overview and Current Legislation, by William J. Mallett, Steven Maguire, and Kevin R. Kosar.

85 U.S. Congress, Senate Committee on Banking, Housing, and Urban Affairs, Testimony of Felix Rohatyn, Co-Chair of the Commission on Public Infrastructure, Hearing on Condition of Our Nation's Infrastructure and Proposals for Needed Improvement, 110th Cong., 2nd Sess., March 11, 2008, http://banking.senate.gov/public/index.cfm?FuseAction=Hearings.Hearing&Hearing_ID=9ddc8203-a3d1-448d-946e-3b1f671fda8a; U.S. Congress, House Committee on Transportation and Infrastructure, Testimony of Bernard Schwartz, President and CEO, BLS Investments, Hearing on Financing Infrastructure Investments, 110th Cong., 2nd Sess., June 10, 2008.

86 U.S. Congress, House Committee of the Budget and Committee on Transportation and Infrastructure, Testimony of Peter R. Orszag, Director, Congressional Budget Office, Hearing on Financing Infrastructure Investment, 110th Cong., 2nd Sess., May 8, 2008.

87 U.S. Congress, House Committee on Ways and Means, Subcommittee on Select Revenue Measures, Testimony of Samuel Staley, Hearing on the National Infrastructure Banks, 111th Cong., 2nd sess., May 13, 2010, http://waysandmeans.house.gov/media/pdf/111/2010May13_Staley_Testimony.pdf.

88 MAP-21 failed to extend authority for states to use federal highway, transit, and rail funds to capitalize a SIB. Bills have been introduced in the 113th Congress to extend this authority (H.R. 3872 and S. 1553).

89 Robert Puentes and Jennifer Thompson, "Banking on Infrastructure: Enhancing State Revolving Funds for Transportation," Brookings Institution, September 2012, http://www.brookings.edu/~/media/research/files/papers/2012/9/12%20state%20infrastructure%20investment%20puentes/12%20state%20infrastructure%20investment%20puentes.pdf.

90 Chicago Investment Trust, http://www.shapechicago.org/.

91 Jeff Frantz, "Dauphin County Creates Infrastructure Bank for Road Improvements," PennLive, March 1, 2013, http://www.pennlive.com/midstate/index.ssf/2013/03/dauphin_county_creates_infrast.html; http://www.dauphincounty.org/government/about-the-county/Pages/News.aspx?NewsID=220.

INDEX

C

D

E

H

I

J

K

L

M

N

O

P

Q

R

S

T

U

V

W